Journal and Letter Book of
Nicholas Buckeridge

A PUBLICATION FROM THE JAMES FORD BELL LIBRARY

AT THE UNIVERSITY OF MINNESOTA

Journal and Letter Book of Nicholas Buckeridge 1651-1654

edited by John R. Jenson

UNIVERSITY OF MINNESOTA PRESS
MINNEAPOLIS

© Copyright 1973 by the University of Minnesota.
All rights reserved.

Published in the United Kingdom and India by the Oxford
University Press, London and Delhi, and in
Canada by the Copp Clark Publishing Co. Limited, Toronto

Library of Congress Catalog Card Number: 73-76896

ISBN 0-8166-0687-0

Preface

The seventeenth-century manuscript journal and letter book of the merchant Nicholas Buckeridge, now in the collection of the James Ford Bell Library, at first glance appears to be written in a language other than English. A photograph of one page, reproduced here following page 83, demonstrates the complexities of both Buckeridge's handwriting and the spelling of the period. The method of transcription followed in this book conforms generally to the plan given by Giles E. Dawson and Laetitia Kennedy-Skipton in their *Elizabethan Handwriting, 1500–1650* (New York, 1966). Buckeridge's spelling and punctuation have been retained, but additional punctuation has been supplied to facilitate the reading of the text. Most abbreviations and contractions have been spelled out, and all superior letters have been lowered without indication. Brackets indicate interpolated material supplied by the editor. Matter deleted by Buckeridge that is of importance to the text is included with a notation that it is crossed out in the original. His interlinear material is added in the appropriate place without notation. It has not been possible to identify a few persons, products, and places. Rather than distract the reader with notations of "unidentified" in the text these have been transcribed without comment.

This volume consists of two parts. In the first, Nicholas Buckeridge is related to the times in general and to the East India Company in particular. A transcription of his journal and letter book, with a short introduction to each part and explanatory notes as needed, forms the main body of the work. It is dated largely in the period 1651 to 1654, containing only two entries of a later date.

The publication of this journal and letter book is important to an understanding of the history of the East India Company in several ways. The period it covers is one for which few records of this kind have survived. Many logbooks and journals of the early years of the Company have been preserved at the India Office but materials for the general period of 1645 to 1660 are scant indeed. The journal also complements the early records of the Assada plantation venture and recounts what is elsewhere found only in the correspondence files of the East India Company. As other journals have done it also gives a picture of the perilous and dangerous life of a merchantman in his endeavors for the Company.

These voyages by Buckeridge were an attempt at beginning a new trade in East Africa and the records of them provide information not previously reported to the East India Company.

I gratefully acknowledge the help and encouragement of Miss Carol Urness and Dr. John Parker of the James Ford Bell Library. Thanks are extended to the Faculty Small Grants Program of the University of Minnesota which enabled me to spend a month in London for research in original documents at the India House Library and the British Museum, and in Oxford at the Bodleian Library. Unpublished Crown copyright material in the India Office Records, Original Correspondence E/3/23, No. 2299, transcribed in the appendix of this book, appears by permission of the Controller of Her Majesty's Stationery Office. The text of MS. Polyglot Or. c. 3 is transcribed in the appendix by permission of the Curators of the Bodleian Library. The assistance provided to me by these institutions was deeply appreciated. Also, a special acknowledgment is due to the University of Minnesota Libraries, for giving me a one-month special duty assignment for the completion of the manuscript.

J. R. J.

Minneapolis, Minnesota
September 1972

Contents

The Setting 3

The Journal and Letter Book 19

Appendixes 89

Index 99

The Setting

The Setting

In 1651 Nicholas Buckeridge set out from India for Madagascar and eastern Africa as a representative of the English East India Company, charged with "Merchandizeing affaires." At the time he was probably in his middle to late twenties; nothing is known about his birth or early years. The name Buckeridge is a common one in England and the family has two main branches: the Buckeridges of Basildon, Berkshire, and those of Pangbourne, Berkshire. The Nicholas Buckeridge of this manuscript was one of seven sons of Arthur Buckeridge of Grandchester, a member of the Basildon branch. One of Nicholas Buckeridge's uncles, John Buckeridge, was the bishop of Ely; he was also a founder of St. John's College, Oxford, and served as its president from 1605 to 1611.

The reason Nicholas Buckeridge decided to make his career with the East India Company is unknown, although a family connection is possible: there are references to an earlier Nicholas Buckeridge as a member of various English trading companies; he was perhaps a relative.[1] A possible reference to our Nicholas Buckeridge is dated 1639, when a man of that name leased property in the small community of Mottingham for twenty years; he rented one of the town's seventeen houses for 5 £ per year.[2] We can only wonder who used this property, if it was our Buckeridge, since he was serving the East India Company abroad in the 1640s and thereafter until the mid-1660s.

Nicholas Buckeridge began his career with the East India Company in the early 1640s. The "Instructions given Us by the President and Councell of India and Persia Unto Mr. Robert Cranmer" dated March 26, 1644, from Surat, notes that Buckeridge is to assist in the management of a voyage to Basra.[3] Francis Breton, the president at Surat, was the author of these instructions. (In the opening years of the overseas administration of the East India Company any trading area could be called a presidency. Later this title was usually reserved for major trade establishments; they were governed by a president who was assisted by a

---

[1] Theodore Rabb, *Enterprise & Empire* (Cambridge, Mass., 1967), p. 192.
[2] Daniel Lysons, *The Environs of London* (London, 1796), vol. IV, p. 419.
[3] India Office Library, Original Correspondence, E/3/19, no. 1865. Hereafter cited as O.C. 1865, etc.

council. Surat became the center of administration for the trade in the Indian Ocean; Madras for that of the eastern Indian trade; Bantam for the trade in the East Indian Archipelago. The governor of the East India Company in London was also called president. William Cockayne was president of the Company from 1643 to 1658; he was assisted by and responsible to a council of twenty-four members.)

Exactly what Buckeridge's position of "assistant" entailed on the 1644 voyage is uncertain, but he obviously was already experienced in trade. The beginning position in foreign service for the Company was that of apprentice, then came writer, factor, junior merchant, senior merchant, councilor, and president or governor. Buckeridge probably acted as some kind of assistant to a factor of the Company. On September 17, 1644, Buckeridge wrote a letter to the president at Surat from Basra, mentioning the arrival of the ships at that port and the goods they brought in.[4] A letter of January 3, 1646, indicates that Buckeridge had "assisted the passed year in our wryting office."[5] It was a practice of the Company to use factors as accountants or copyists when they were not employed at sea, so this does not indicate that Buckeridge was in the writer class. On March 30, 1646, he was on the ship *Francis* bound for Mocha. He and a Mr. Joseph Cross reported to the Company that they had continued on from Mocha to "Delieka, Swakaine, and Mussora" (Dahlak Island, Suakin, and Massawa). On December 2, 1646, Buckeridge was on a journey inland from Mocha, this time by camel caravan to the town of Ta'izz. The journey was not successful, for much of the cloth was ruined en route and was not salable. Both Mr. Cross and Buckeridge were ill, and Mr. Cross died on December 31. Buckeridge was "sich of feavers" — probably malaria, though it may have been any of the diseases that claimed the lives of so many East India Company men through the years. A report on this trading venture was written to the Company on January 16, 1646/47.[6] (Hereafter old-style dates will be written according to present usage e.g., January 16, 1647.)

East India employees often found themselves confronted with problems of local diplomacy. Buckeridge, for one, in a voyage in 1647 from Mocha to Aden, found that he had to contend not only with the problems of poor markets for trade but also with an irate governor. The governor of Aden became angry over the activities of Buckeridge's

---

[4] O.C. 1891.
[5] O.C. 1970.
[6] O.C. 1998.

INDIAN OCEAN

partner, John Totty, who had tried to force incoming Malabar ships to buy passes from him before being allowed to trade with the local merchants. Totty sailed his ship back and forth in the harbor, firing his guns and causing a general disturbance. The governor summoned Buckeridge and threatened to make him a prisoner and to seize the Company's goods if Totty did not change his attitude. Buckeridge sent word to Totty and persuaded him to stop his actions. All seems to have been resolved: Totty begged Buckeridge's forgiveness and offered apologies to the governor, the Malabar ships were allowed to trade, and the Company's ships were permitted to depart. The Company suffered a loss because of this incident, for merchants on their way to Aden on hearing of the disturbance there went to Mocha instead to conduct business.[7] In 1649 Buckeridge was back in Surat and listed on the payroll of the factory there.

That Buckeridge made still another visit to Mocha is substantiated by the "Instructions Given by Us ye president & Councell unto Mr Nicholas Buckeridge bound upon Pinnance Lannarett for Mocha and thence to Swakin in Negotiation of the Companys affaires in that place."[8] It is clear from these instructions that Buckeridge is an experienced traveler to these ports, for he is to advise Mr. Wylde, the master, in any way he can regarding goods to be sold, prices to ask, and so forth. When Buckeridge departs, he is to leave instructions for Wylde "because yow [Buckeridge] have better experience (gained by former employments in those affaires) than Mr Wylde etc. who are strangers to such actions."

A letter of April 8, 1651, is the first document in the correspondence of the East India Company linking the ship *Assada Merchant* with Nicholas Buckeridge. In that letter the *Assada Merchant* is cited as being the only ship which has not returned from her current voyage. By the time of her arrival "we shall have in readiness a small Cargo . . . of Cloth provideing at Cambaya, and rise, heere bought, with which we intend . . . shee shall voyage to ye Coast of Malinda (and on hir Nicholas Buckeridg for ye Merchandizeing affaires) to experiment ye marketts on that coast."[9] That voyage is the first one recorded in the journal and letter book transcribed in this book.

In 1651 England was still trying to secure its hold on trade in the Indian Ocean. The Portuguese had dominated the eastern trade in the decades following the voyage of Vasco da Gama to India in the fifteenth century. Da Gama's round-trip journey had encompassed some 3800 miles, the greatest feat of navigation to his day. Later generations of traders followed this arduous route and went still further to the East. In da Gama's voyage over half the crew was lost, and this pattern, too, persisted in later voyages. Scurvy, dysentery, malaria, unknown tropical diseases — all were part of the price of eastern voyages. Still, the profits obtained were felt to be worth the extraordinary cost.

The Portuguese originally went to the East for spices and silk. They discovered, however, that there was a profitable carrying trade in the Indian Ocean as well. They pushed the Arab traders out and imported

---

[7] India Office Library, Factory Records, Surat, G/36/102A, pp. 127, 129.
[8] Bodleian Library, Oxford, MS. Eng. Hist. c. 63, folios 54ff.
[9] O.C. 2216.

calico and beads from India to exchange in Africa for gold and ivory, in later years for slaves. The trade was essentially a coastal one, and the Portuguese made no attempt to penetrate into the interior of either Africa or India, with the exception of the establishment of Sena, about a hundred miles inland on the Zambezi River in Africa. The Portuguese empire, in theory, stretched from the Cape of Good Hope to the Far East. The Portuguese tried to hold a monopoly on trade in that area but could not keep other Europeans out of it. Spices were obtained at Malabar and the Moluccas, horses at Ormuz, cinnamon at Ceylon, textiles from Gujarat and Coromandel, and silks and silver from China and Japan. The chief coastal trade in Africa was in ivory, ambergris, tortoiseshells, slaves, wax, millet, and rice, purchased principally with cotton cloth from India. The discovery of Brazil turned Portuguese interests toward the New World, and in addition, the annexation of Portugal by Spain in 1580 amalgamated Portuguese interests into those of the Spanish empire. Portugal was no longer the predominant power in the East.

The Dutch were also after a share of eastern trade. Following several independent Dutch voyages, in 1602 the Vereenigde Oost-Indische Compagnie (United East India Company) was chartered. This company was granted exclusive rights of trade to the East Indies by the Cape of Good Hope route, and was empowered to make treaties, raise troops, build fortresses, appoint officials, and in general exercise almost unlimited power, in the name of the state. The first fleet of the new company set sail in the spring of 1602. Its objectives were to gain a firm foothold in the East Indies and to harass the Portuguese there. The Dutch found it to their advantage to use a few places as bases for trade operations and extend their influence from these to adjoining areas. As had the Portuguese, the Dutch, too, became involved in the inter-Asiatic trade, particularly that between the Indian Ocean and the China Sea. It was inevitable that the Dutch would clash with the English who were also bent on trade in the East.

The English had long dreamed of eastern trade. In 1581 the Levant Company had been formed, to open an overland route to the East. It managed to bring Indian goods back to England, but more importantly, it brought back information on the rich trading possibilities there. But the overland route was costly and dangerous; English merchants could not compete with the Dutch, who were sailing to eastern ports. By the end of the sixteenth century the price of pepper had almost tripled because of the Dutch monopoly, and the English yearned to get into pepper trade.

The defeat of the Spanish Armada seemed to signal that the time was ripe, and as early as 1589 English merchants asked the queen for permission to send ships to the Indies. Three ships were sent out. The experiment was a complete disaster, but the survivors provided enough information to encourage future schemes. The East India Company was chartered on December 31, 1600. The charter was signed by Queen Elizabeth to ". . . the members of the Company, their sons, of the age of twenty-one years, and their apprentices, factors, and servants, [who] were authorized to carry on trade to the East-Indies (that is, to all countries beyond the Cape of Good Hope, to the Straits of Magellan), for fifteen years, from Christmas 1600, provided that such trade should not be to any place in possession of any Christian prince in amity with the Queen, who should publicly declare his objection thereto . . ."[10] Much of the capital of the Company came from members of the Levant Company.

The first fleet of the newly formed East India Company sailed in 1601. Four ships made the trip to Sumatra, where a factory was established at Achin, and went on to Bantam. They returned to England in 1603 to find Queen Elizabeth had been succeeded by King James, who was not sympathetic to the monopoly of the East India Company. In 1609, contrary to the original patent of Elizabeth, he granted trading rights to another group. These were the first so-called "interlopers." The interlopers provided English competition for the East India Company in addition to that already being felt from the Portuguese and the Dutch in the East Indies. Conferences were held in 1613 and 1615 between the Dutch and the English in an attempt to reach an agreement about eastern trade. The English profited from these conferences by learning much about the organization of the Dutch East India Company. On July 17, 1619, a treaty was finally signed as the result of a third conference. The English were to have one-third of the East Indies trade, the Dutch two-thirds, with the treaty to remain in effect for twenty years. It proved impossible to enforce.

The infamous "Amboina Massacre" in February 1623 destroyed any possibility of further cooperation between the Dutch and the English. Amboina, the main island of a group having the same name, had been a center for the Portuguese clove monopoly until the Dutch East India Company took over the trade there in 1605. In 1615 the English began to trade on the same island; under the treaty of 1619 they were to be al-

---

[10] John Bruce, *Annals of the Honourable East-India Company*, 3 vols. (London, 1810), vol. I, p. 136.

lowed one-third of the trade and were to pay one-third of the cost of the fort there. Early in 1623, one of the Japanese mercenary soldiers on the island was accused of spying for the English and he confessed to it. The other Japanese soldiers were arrested. An Englishman was also tortured and he "confessed" that the English were planning a takeover of the fort. The Dutch then arrested all Englishmen in the Moluccas, tortured them, and hanged ten of them, along with ten Japanese soldiers and one Portuguese. The Amboina tragedy marked the end of English trade in the East Indian Archipelago in that period. English merchants concentrated instead on an area within easier reach, the Indian Ocean.

The English began trading on the west coast of India in 1612, though still opposed by the Portuguese. English merchants were well received at Surat, and the king gave permission for the settlement of an English factory there in December of the same year. Trade with Persia was begun in 1618, after Sir Thomas Roe had gone as ambassador to the Great Mogul to obtain concessions for English trade. Before Roe left India in February 1619, the English East India Company had established factories at Surat, Agra, Ahmadabad, and Broach, all of which were placed under the control of the president and council of the Surat factory.

Indian textiles were much in demand in the trade of the Persian Gulf. As the reader of the Buckeridge journal and letter book will note, there was "a bewildering variety of names for the different types of cloth manufactured at the time."[11] All the varieties, however, may be classified under two main headings: piece goods and ready-made clothing. Piece goods were sold either by the "piece" of conventional size or by the "corge," that is, a score of pieces. The cloth was a plain cotton, brown, bleached, or dyed red or blue. The two chief varieties were calico, a strong cloth, and muslin, a much thinner type. Ready-made clothing, which involved little tailoring, was also made of calico and muslin, but unlike piece goods was generally patterned. The patterns were produced at times by the use of colored yarns, but it was more common to print the design with wooden blocks or paint it on the cloth with a pen. The printed variety was known as chintz, the painted variety as pintadoes or simply "painted" cloth. There were three chief sources of supply of these Indian textiles in the seventeenth century: Gujarat, Coromandel, and Bengal. The Coromandel coast was the best source of supply for the English.

---

[11] Tapan Raychaudhuri, *Jan Company in Coromandel, 1605–1690* (The Hague, 1962), p. 10.

On his first voyage from India to east Africa in 1651, Buckeridge was instructed to leave letters of information for ships due to arrive from England regarding the demise of the colony at Assada. The Assada scheme had its birth in 1635, when a grant for trade in the Indies was given to Sir William Courten. In 1636 William Courten died; the East India Company hoped to prevent the renewal of his charter, but in 1637 a new charter was granted to a son, also Sir William Courten. The Courten Company was restricted to areas where the "old Company" (East India Company) was not established; in turn, the East India Company was instructed not to attempt trade where the Courten Company was operating. The competition between the two was intense. In 1645 three ships of the Courten Company with about 150 colonists were sent out to Madagascar to establish a colony. The first choice for its location was Augustine Bay, but a better place was searched for, with Nossi Bé (Assada Island) discovered as a possible later location. The next ship that went to Augustine Bay found the colony in near ruins; the few survivors were picked up and taken to India or the Comoro Islands. In 1649 a second attempt was made. This time, under the leadership of Colonel Robert Hunt, several ships sailed to establish a plantation at Assada. The *Assada Merchant*, later to be Nicholas Buckeridge's ship, was one of them. The colony held out for several months but it too had to be disbanded and the survivors were taken to Surat where they were given the opportunity to enter East India Company service.

The Courten Company employees in Madagascar had aroused considerable hatred among the local people by coining fake pagodas and rials. The India merchants did not distinguish between the two companies and vented their displeasure on the East India Company. This led to pressure in London to abolish the Courten Company and in January 1650 a United Joint Stock Company was formed which combined the operations of the two companies.

The Dutch and English competition often led to open hostility, and Buckeridge asks in a report of 1653, section VI in this book, "whither wee have warr or Peace with holland & Portugall or either of them that wee may regulate ourselvs accordingly." The Dutch and English were at war from 1652 to 1654, but the news of it did not reach Surat until March 1653. The war was precipitated by many years of Dutch interference with English trade in the East and by the English Navigation Act of 1651 which was aimed at limiting imports to those carried in English ships. The war, fought entirely at sea in a series of twelve fleet actions, affected the trade in the East only slightly. The Dutch blockaded the port of Surat but then sailed for the Persian Gulf. There in a battle three ships of the English East India Company were captured and one was run aground and destroyed. A treaty of peace was signed April 5, 1654.

The record of Nicholas Buckeridge's activities at the time of the war indicates he was little affected by it. There are some gaps in information as transcribed here from the journal and letter book. From September 11, 1651, the end of the first voyage recorded, to December 13, 1652, the date the second was begun, there is no information about his life. A letter of January 10, 1652, gives a general résumé of the operation of the East India Company, however, and does offer some background information. That letter states that the *Assada Merchant* traded in Mozambique and returned on October 12, 1651, to Surat.[12] The ship apparently was sent down the coast of India on a short trip to Batticaloa in Ceylon. During this period Buckeridge was probably employed in Surat on Company business, perhaps as an accountant or copyist, though he would seem to have been too valuable an employee for such a position.

Buckeridge went on a second voyage to East Africa in search of markets from the middle of December 1652 to November 30, 1653, when he returned to Bassein. From that time until March 1656, there is no information about him, though it can again be assumed that he was working for the Company at Surat. A Court of Committees report dated March 12, 1656, lists eight persons who are to "remain" and "continue" at Surat, among them Nicholas Buckeridge.[13] In April of the same year he left on the *Assada Merchant* for "Bantam Macassar, etta." He is identified as one who "is cheife manager of this voiage."[14] The *Assada Merchant* has had several unfortunate voyages; Buckeridge has hopes that "his Melinda fortune does not persue him, for this vessel never yet hardly made a good voiage for your Account." But this voyage, too, was plagued by mishaps. Bad weather prevented the ship from stopping at Makassar and she did not arrive in Bantam until sometime in May. Trading there was not successful, apparently because some of the goods taken were not suitable for the trade and some were ruined in transport. A series of accusations and rebuttals passed between Buckeridge and others in the Company who were involved.[15] In February 1657 Buckeridge wrote that the *Assada Merchant* could not trade at Bantam because

---

[12] O.C. 2228.
[13] Court Minutes, B/25, vol. 23, p. 502.
[14] O.C. 2545.
[15] O.C. 2566, 2567, 2568, 2569, 2570, 2571, 2573, 2580, 2583, 2585, 2586.

of Dutch opposition; the Company's goods were to be taken to Batavia instead. In July the *Assada Merchant* was ordered to Cambodia to pick up the Company's goods and all persons employed there. The factory in Cambodia was closed and abandoned.[16]

In 1658 Buckeridge was again ordered to service at Surat. "The Companies business requiring an able man, at the Marin . . . we can pitch upon none fitter for ye Imployment then your selfe."[17] The difficulties of the previous year seemingly had no adverse effect upon his reputation so far as the Company was concerned. His stay at Surat was short, for in April 1658 Buckeridge received an appointment as a representative of the Company in Persia because of "the good opinion which wee have conceived of your abilities and experiences hat [sic] caused us to make choice off, and to enterteyne you into our Imployment for your manadgment of our affaires in Persia . . ."[18] This was not a new field of endeavor for Buckeridge, for, as we have seen, he had been employed there some eighteen years earlier. William Garway was appointed agent; Nicholas Buckeridge and two other men were to serve as a council "that they together joyntly act, and manadge all our affaires . . ." In the event of the death of Mr. Garway, Buckeridge was given the authority to succeed him as agent.

Early in 1659 Buckeridge was back in Surat briefly, and from there he returned to Persia. From Gombroon Buckeridge advised the Company about the best goods to send for marketing there.[19] He wanted to leave his position as agent of the Company in Persia, and two men were sent out to replace him. Unfortunately both of them died; Buckeridge himself had been ill. On June 7, 1660, Buckeridge wrote, "My fortune is not soe good as to bee sent for home now, yett to have any body with me live that ffitting to Resigne to. I obliged to serve but one yeare & 2 are past already. I intend god willing to leave this place next May. I shall be glad to serve you in meane time . . ."[20]

Finally, after many years of Company service abroad, Buckeridge came home. The Company in London reported simply that "Mr Buckeridge is safely arrived with us . . . 24 Mar 1662."[21] The next year several Courts of Committee meetings were held about estates and out-

---

[16] O.C. 2632.
[17] Factory Records, Surat, G/36/84, p. 229.
[18] Factory Records, Miscellaneous, G/40/3, vol. 3, pp. 97-99.
[19] O.C. 2730.
[20] O.C. 2850.
[21] Dispatch Books, E/3/86, p. 249.

standing business relating to Buckeridge. Settlements apparently were made in his favor, for a number of payments of some several hundred pounds each were authorized.[22]

Buckeridge did not stay in London long. On December 16, 1663, he received his "commission and instructions" to go to the East again. He was sent on the ship *Happy Entrance* to Madras, as an investigator to examine the records, survey the operations, and report to the Company on its business operations there. The instructions noted that "it will be very necessary that you keep a Dyary of all your proceedings, duely and daiely entring therein all necessary occurences and Passages during this your intended voyage in all places, which Booke at your Retorne, we expect you shall deliver unto us, and therefore we desire you to observe this our Order and performe accordingly."[23] Buckeridge was to return on one of the last ships laded for England the next year. That he did keep such a journal, as East India Company officials were often required to do, is probable, but it has not survived.

Buckeridge evidently went on a number of these inspection trips. In October 1664 he was in Madras again, investigating the conduct of a Company servant there,[24] and in August 1665 he wrote that he had visited Verasharoone "and finde your ffactory there much out of repair . . ."[25] He said he had traveled much in the past year: January 5 sailed from Metchlapatam; January 8 arrived at Madras; January 12 set sail; April 3 passed Cape of Good Hope; April 25 arrived at St. Helena; May 10 sailed for England; July 26 stopped at Fiall Island for provisions; July 31 sailed again for England; August 18 arrived at the English Channel. The letter citing these travels is dated "Ship Rebecca at Sea Aug ye 19th 1665."

Sometime after his return to London in 1662, Buckeridge had married Miss Sarah Bainbridge, daughter of William Bainbridge, a merchant of St. Giles-in-the-Fields, London. William Bainbridge owned acres of land in that area; streets there were named after him and after three of his sons-in-law: Nicholas Buckeridge, William Maynard, and Simon Dyott.[26] Stow described Buckeridge Street as "on the West side of Dyot Street, another narrow and ordinary Place, which falls into St. Giles by

---

[22] Court Book, vol. 24, p. 709.
[23] Dispatch Books, E/3/86, pp. 348–351.
[24] Factory Records, Fort St. George, G/19/15, pp. 83ff.
[25] O.C. 3064 + 1.
[26] London, County Council, *Survey of London*, vol. V, part II: *The Parish of St. Giles-in-the-Fields* (London, 1914), p. 145.

the Pound; and is over against Hog Lane."[27] Buckeridge Street is no longer in existence; it was destroyed with the building of New Oxford Street 1847. Dyott, Maynard, and Bainbridge streets can still be seen.

Buckeridge and his wife had five children: Bainbridge (born in 1668), Sarah (who married Matthew May in 1707), Jane (who married William Bourne), and Elizabeth. The family at first lived in the parish of St. Christopher le Stocks. In 1670 Buckeridge signed a seventy-one-year lease for "soe much ground as can conveniently be spared out of the passage on ye North side of the Church at the rate of Sixpence p foote square p an."[28] Buckeridge and his family did not, however, remain near St. Christopher le Stocks long; in 1675 they, with Buckeridge's wife's sisters and their husbands, settled in the manor of Bury cum Hepmangrove in Huntingdonshire. This arrangement proved to be short-lived also, and the three couples sold that property the following year.[29]

Buckeridge returned to his property near St. Christopher le Stocks, and in 1678 he signed an entry in the vestry book of that parish. In 1681 the parish had a special assessment "to be paid yearely by Quarterly Payments in Liew of Tythes to the Parson of the said Parish . . ."[30] Members of the parish are listed geographically; item forty-one is "Nicholas Buckeridge, Church Alley next the church doore." His assessment was 17s 4d.[31]

An ecclesiastical history of the diocese of London, published in 1708, states, "there are no Enchroachments made upon the Church St. Christopher le Stocks Church-yard, or Glebe except of one small irregular pice of the Church-yard, which is taken into a house or houses of one Nicolas Buckeridge, of which there is a Lease granted (now in the Churchwardens Hands) from the Parson and the Churchwardens, and at the annual Rent of 3 £ 2s 6d."[32] The church is no longer in existence;

---

[27] John Stow, *A Survey of the Cities of London and Westminster. Corrected, improved and very much enlarged by John Strype* (London, 1720), vol. 2, p. 85.
[28] London, St. Christopher le Stocks (Parish), *Minutes of the Vestry Meetings and Other Records of the Parish of St. Christopher le Stocks in the City of London*, edited by Edwin Freshfield (London, 1886), p. 52.
[29] *The Victoria History of the Counties of England: Huntingdonshire*, edited by William Page, Granville Proby, and S. Inskip Ladds, 4 vols. (London, 1932), vol. II, p. 164.
[30] St. Christopher le Stocks, *Minutes*, p. 60.
[31] St. Christopher le Stocks, *Minutes*, p. 76.
[32] Richard Newcourt, *Repertorium ecclesiasticum Parochiale Londinense: An ecclesiastical Parochial history of the Diocease of London*, 2 vols. (London, 1708), vol. 1, p. 232.

the property is now covered by the western wing of the Bank of England, part of the churchyard forming an internal court.

There are no records of the death of Nicholas Buckeridge, but it probably occurred sometime in 1688 or 1689. The latter year his son, Bainbridge, wrote the note found at the end of the journal and letter book transcribed below: "Ye end of my fathers Letters in this book. B B 1689." Two other manuscripts of Nicholas Buckeridge's survive. In 1691 Bainbridge noted in a manuscript now in the Bodleian Library that it was "Collected by my father in his residence in Persia & the Indies anno 1640." [33] Another manuscript at the Bodleian is inscribed "Some writings belonging to Nicholas Buckeridge . . . collected without any regard had to method or ye Order in which they were wrote, B. B. 1713." [34] A further note on the first Bodleian manuscript indicates "this book belongs to mr. Buckeridge Gentleman Commoner of St. Johns: but perhaps he may leave it to the Library." Madan suggests that Bainbridge Buckeridge probably gave the manuscript to the Bodleian soon after 1700.[35]

The manuscript transcribed here may be described physically as follows. It is covered with dark brown calf, 19½ × 14½ cm. There is no lettering or decoration other than two lines of blind stamping in each direction. Holes in the front and back cover on the outer foredge indicate that at one time there were ties to hold the volume closed. The paper, 18¾ × 14 cm., contains a watermark known to be used in paper of the 1640s.[36] Several numbering systems have been employed by various owners through the years since the manuscript was written. Beginning with the first page of text the pages are numbered at the bottom in pencil, 1–108; a second numbering appears on the top verso pages, 1–54. A few of the latter are in ink in Buckeridge's hand; the rest are in pencil. The manuscript is divided into sections by penciled Roman numerals. A ¾ blank leaf between 15 and 16 is not numbered, but 17, also a blank, is numbered. Following folio 54, which carries the note in Bainbridge Buckeridge's hand, there is the stub of a torn-out page and two blank leaves.

---

[33] Bodleian Library, Oxford, MS Bod. 51.
[34] Bodleian Library, Oxford, MS Eng. Hist. c. 63.
[35] Falconer Madan and H. H. E. Craster, *A Summary Catalog of Western Manuscripts in the Bodleian Library at Oxford* (Oxford, 1895–1953), Entry 27766.
[36] William A. Churchill, *Watermarks in Paper in Holland, England, France, etc., in the XVII and XVIII Centuries and Their Interconnection* (Amsterdam, 1935), p. CCCXLVI, figure 469.

The Journal and Letter Book

The Journal and Letter Book

I

The first section of the journal and letter book is a record of the earliest voyage made by Nicholas Buckeridge to Madagascar and East Africa. This voyage had been planned as early as November 15, 1650, when a council of East India Company officials decided to send the *Assada Merchant* to Madagascar following her return from a trip to Gombroon. A letter of November 19 from the president of the Company in Surat mentions that one of the objectives of the planned trip was to deposit letters at Augustine Bay with details about the abandonment of the Assada plantation. (See above, page 10.) Another letter, dated January 31, 1651, reveals an uncertainty whether the expedition will trade only at Persia, Mocha, and Bussora or will "send ye Assadoe to ye Coast of Malinda, for a tryall of which wee have not yet absolutely resolved." Finally, a letter of April 8, 1651, to the Company notes that the *Assada Merchant* "shall voyage to ye Coast of Malinda (and on hir Nicholas Buckridg, for ye Merchandizeing affaires) to experiment ye marketts on that coast." The ship returned from Gombroon April 16 and sailed for East Africa thirteen days later, on April 29, 1651; it arrived at Swally Marine (Surat) on October 11, 1651.[1]

Many details regarding the *Assada Merchant* can be gleaned from reports and letters sent to the East India Company in London. The pinnace was a small vessel propelled with oars and sails of two or three masts, schooner-rigged, carvel-built like a barge but smaller, with a flat stern. It was used as a merchant ship but also could be converted for use in war. O.C. 2179 gives a description: ". . . the ship seemed well at distance but when wee went on board wee found hir a very ill shapen, and Contrived vessell, shee hath two decks, where of hir Gun deck is not above

---

[1] See O.C. 2181, 2182, 2204, 2216, 2228.

4 foote high, at ye most, hir hold very small, hir two Bulk heades not distant about 4 ordinary strides one from an other, (noe Cabin but only a round house) and reckoned by the master of the ffaulcon and hir cheife Carpenter whom wee tooke downe to veiw hir not to be above 100 tons of burthen, her maine mast soe rotten for neare the one third parte, from the topp of it, that it Crumbles to pieces as dirt which wee are in repaireing, and fitting hir other wise, for A Gombroone voyage . . ." Buckeridge mentions that a skiff and a long boat were used. He also notes later in his journal that the ship was shorthanded, having only sixteen men on the return trip to India in 1653. She had a limited capacity; O.C. 2204 describes the *Assada Merchant* as sailing with a cargo of sixty-three bales of "several sortes of Goods" and in O.C. 2216 it is said that "we shall have in readiness a small cargo (but in bulke as much as we doe esteeme hir Capable to receive)." The *Assada Merchant*, along with the *Seahorse*, is referred to in O.C. 2228 as "of very small capassity." O.C. 2504 records that she was sold in 1655 because it would cost too much to repair her. (The new owner, however, did repair the ship and continued using her for many more years.)

The portion of the manuscript that follows begins with the arrival of the *Assada Merchant* in Mozambique on July 15, 1651, and continues through September 11, 1651. Buckeridge is most concerned with making a full report of his customs problems in Mozambique. He also gives a general port-by-port résumé of trade.

July ye 15th 1651

15th Pinnace Assada Marchant came to an Anchor in Mosambiq Roade, about one A Clock in the afternoone, in 9½ ffadam [i.e., fathom] water, foule ground [i.e., rocky, shallow, or otherwise dangerous for anchorage], some 5 or 6 Miles of[f] of the Chastle, under St. James his Island.[2] Whence I went Ashore in ye Shipps boat to the governer acquainting him

---

[2] Olfert Dapper, in his *Description de l'Afrique*, 1686, describes this "Chastle," or fort, at the end of Mozambique Island as being less well made than other Portuguese forts elsewhere along the coast, and says that it was square with canons commanding the entrance to the inner harbor and the village. Three islands are located at the mouth of the Magincate River: Mozambique, the largest, St. George, and St. James. The last is an uninhabited island which lies to the south of Mozambique.

with the intent of our comeinge & deliveringe him ye Presidents Letter³ to ye same effect, which when hee had perused [it], hee tould me hee must take Councell with others about ye matter & would send me his answer on board to morrow, & now I might goe Abord. & soe dispatched me, with out any other Ceremonie or enterteinment saveing that in A Complement he tould me their Chastle was at my service. & soe I returned not haveinge been ½ an hower ashore & got abord againe before 5 A clock. Before I went Ashore the Master tould me that hee darst not ride with out [since] ye ground was soe foule & that if we were to dispatch any business that would requirer stay, the Shipp must goe in. Wher upon ye governer Askinge me whether we determined to bring ye Shipp in, seeming strange that wee road with out, I tould him wee planed not to come with out his leave.

Mozambiq July 16th 1651

16th In the morninge by breake of day came a boate of[f] from ye governer with A Letter (which endeavoured to come last night but could not) intemateing their willingnesse to trade with us, inviteinge us in, saying they were ready with open Armes to inbrace us. Further the bearer tould me that the governer imediatly upon my leaveinge him assembled the Cheife inhabitants of the toune to consult with, who instantly relolved [sic] to trade with us. Her upon we held A Consultation & resolved to goe in under Commaund; there beinge A necessitie for it. Inquieringe of some Indean Laskars [i.e., East Indian sailors] that rowed ye Boat abord which ye governers Letter came in, they tould us that noe Customs are paid here, & inquireing for news, they tould us of A Portugall vessell bound from Choule⁴ to this place puttinge in for Assada⁵ by

---

³ This letter was an official request for trading privileges from the president of the East India Company at Surat.
⁴ Chaul (Chowle, Chaoul, Choule), just south of Bombay, was an especially important seaport in western India in the sixteenth century because of its excellent position for receiving ships from Malabar and Cambay. It was famous for silks.
⁵ Maps of Madagascar from this period — for example, the François

ye way was treacherouslie carried away by the Laskars, who masakared all ye Portugalls that were in her, being about 35. Ye reason that moved them to this attempt was as as [*sic*] these Laskars report occasioned by an abuse offered them by ye Portugalls at Sea, who in contempt of them & their superstition, put Swines fflesh into their water, in revenge whereof they accted Soe perfideous A Tragedy. Mr Mathew wood in Shipp welcome (I since understand it was Captain strong in Ship recovery) arrivinge there very Shortlie after this mischief so was effected.[6] Thay have agreed with him for 10000 Pardos[7] (to go in quest of her) if hee can take her & he is gon after her towards the red Sea whither tis supposed they are gonne & hath taken one Portugall with him which knowes ye vessell. We came into the ye [*sic*] iner Roade under Comaund about noone, where wee found Rideinge A great Shipp from Lisboa named the Nazarite, who loosinge her Monzoones spent much time in [crossed out: ye River of Quilean leying in upwards of 20 degrees] Angola & hath been here some 3 Months [i.e., because seasonal winds had stopped or become

---

Cauche map of 1657 and the Nicholas Sanson map of 1655 — do not show Assada. The Sanson map does have some unnamed islands in the general area. Blaeu's map of 1663 shows the northern end of Madagascar as "Pays incogneu." Flacourt, in his history of Madagascar, 1657, omits any mention of Assada. Charles Wylde's "Journal of the Ship Bonitto," 1650–1652 (in the James Ford Bell Library), provides full descriptions, maps, and soundings for Assada. A note after the last entry in that journal indicates the manuscript was used as a guide for a voyage as late as 1740.

[6] Because of the desertion of the Assada settlement, Captain Peter Strong, commander of the *Recovery*, continued on to Surat. The *Recovery* is listed as a "small private vessel." She sailed on her return voyage near the end of October 1651, was in St. Helena on April 27, 1652, and reached England on July 29, 1652. As master of the ship *Welcome*, Wood had been paid fifty shillings per head for transporting thirteen of the planters from the Assada plantation to India. There is no evidence that he was able to collect the money offered him to capture the Laskars. He died of a fever about a month after arriving at Diu in India. The *Welcome* landed at Madraspatam, India, on July 4, 1651, and returned to England in 1652. Buckeridge had later found that it was not the *Welcome* and inserted a correction in the margin of the manuscript.

[7] A pardao was a coin used in Goa. At the end of the sixteenth century it was worth about 4s 6d, but its value afterward diminished. It was equal to 360 reis or rials of gold or 300 reis of silver.

unstable, the ship was unable to continue and had to wait for the next monsoon season]. 2 other of her Companions went hence for Goa.[8] In May last, from Indea here arrived 4 vessells from Goa: 1, from Inden, ye Chowle vessell, miscarried as prementioned & ye reason why ye Damon[9] vessell came not, I knew at Surratt[10] viz ye displaceing of ye old Captain when his vessell was ready to come away. About noone I went A shore to ye Governer & was Courteouslie enterteined by him & hee promised to bee merchant for ye greatest part of our goods himselfe & urged me to tell ye Quantitie, which I pretended was some 40: or 50: Bales Cloth, & some Rice. To which hee gave smale Creditt, sayinge hee wanted more then that Quantitie for his owne occasiones & desired me to bring ashore ye musters [i.e., samples of goods] & A list of ye particulars of what we had & all the marchants would meete to morrow morninge at his howse where we should make a gratt bargaine for all, which I agreed to. & desireing his leave to take A howse, hee was Unwillinge thereto, tellinge mee of much danger in Robery & fier & that if wee went through with our bargain I should not neede one, soe I urged it noe ffurther conceiveinge hee did it in policie to keep mee in ignorance of ye prizes of goods till ye bargain was made. To prevent which I imployed Gosse to inquier among ye Laskars of ye valiue of goods which by theire relation was very good & that there was a scarcitie of goods in towne — by reason of ye Choule Vesells miscariage & other Vesells not comeinge this yeare. & inquieringe further about Customes I

---

[8] Goa was the most important port of the East. It was the seat of Portuguese government there and a center for all Portuguese commercial activities. It had a deep, safe harbor and good anchoring ground. The harbor was protected by a large battery of guns and by forts and it was regarded as the strongest harbor in India.

[9] Daman (Damon, Damão) is a seaport in western India on the Gulf of Cambay, located at the mouth of the Damanganga River 100 miles north of Bombay. It was annexed by the Portuguese in 1559.

[10] Surat is situated near the mouth of the Tapti River, about 150 miles north of Bombay. The first English factory in India was founded there in 1612. From this beginning, Surat continued as the seat of British Indian government until 1687. Its location was important because several rivers from inland India converged there and goods could easily be brought to the coast for trade.

was informed that Customs are not paid here, but ye Agreement is made for that in Indea — which somewhat troubles me that I am not resolved what to trust to, herin haveing wilfully omitted mentioning thereof at my being with the governer in regaurd of ye first report, conceiveing it A thing inpertinent to move such A thing to bring it to their mindes if it were not accustomary.

Mosambiq: July ye 17th 1651

17th   This Morning I sent ye Governer A present by Gossee vizt:

- 1 Chist Rosewater [11] 200 bott
- 1 Bag Almonds: 5 mn: Gombroon
- 4: Loavs Luckno Sugar [12] 75 lb
- 2: holland Cheeses

and sent not the Chist of wine conceiveing it inproper in respect hee is soe plentifully supplied with Lisborn wine. & accordinge to promise I Carried ashore musters of the goods, but not comeing soe early as hee expected hee sent for me. Being come hee had assembled the marchants & they veiued ye goods & prized them which I held high. Hearing that ye marketts were good I gave him notice of 50 Bales Cloth: 30 whereof wer Paups,[13] ye Comodity hee wanted & in fine I perceive that till I have sould him them noe thinge elce is to bee donne. His higest price is 5 Xados [14] in Eliphants teeth

---

[11] Rosewater was obtained by distillation from red or damask roses. It was much esteemed in Europe as a good cordial, but later was used only for treating diseases of the eyes, in perfumes, and in washes. It was well received throughout the East, particularly in China and Persia.

[12] Little sugar was available on the Malabar coast, since the chief sources of it were Agra and Lucknow, in northern India.

[13] Byrampauts (beiramee, byramee, byrams) was a cotton cloth much traded during the period when exporting of cloth from India flourished. Its exact definition is not known, as is the case with many other terms used for cotton piece goods. It seems to have been a very fine material.

[14] A xado, i.e., crusado, was a Portuguese coin bearing the figure of a cross, originally of gold, later of silver. It was worth about 400 reis or about 4 English shillings.

at price Currentt, which is 260: Xados: per Bahar,[15] which I fear I must yeild to though they be worth above 6: Xzados to be sould in towne.

18 This day I profered him ½ ye Quantitie at his owne price conditionally I might make my best marketts of ye others, ½ which hee would not consent to, nither let me tak a house to sell Anything elce till hee had made that bargain. Wher upon I proffered them for 5½ but cannot bring him to it. But hee saith to morrow wee shall make A Bargain. But it must be, I perceive, how hee please. But I have this day obteined his promise to bee free from all duties if I will make an end of this bargain.

19th In the morninge I concluded A Bargain with ye Governer for 30 Bales 900 Corge [score, i.e., twenty] Paups at 5¼- Xsados per corge in Murteen [ivory?] at price Currentt & tooke his leave to hier A howse to sell our other goods in. & goeing to veiu one I mett a man which I toke to be a Sariant [i.e., servant?] who delivered mee A note from ye Pre Rectore of ye Jesuits here, declareinge that I must pay 1000 Xados for ye Don owner of these voyages in Goa whose ffactor hee was or I must not land any goods here, to which I Answered that I would advise with ye Governer & returne ye Padry an answer. Wher upon I went to ye Governer & acquainted him therewith who tould me that such A duty there was, but would not amount to soe much, but I must Compound as well as I could & hee would assist me ther in, wher upon I desired him to send for the Padry & Conclude it, which hee did & spoke much in our behalfe. But ye Jesuit would not Conclude with out further information & advice, pretending ye discharge of his trust with fidelitie & to carry an even hand in reason betweene both, wher upon ye Governer bid me advise with him & others & afterwards hee would end the businesse. Soe askinge ye Jesuit when I should waight upon him, hee tould me anytime tomorrow, which I

---

[15] The bahar (barre, bah) was a measure of weight used in parts of India and China, varying in value in different locations from 223 to 625 pounds. Spices were weighed by "great bahar" which equaled 550 pounds, Portuguese; "small bahar" was equal to 401 lb. 7 oz., Portuguese.

refused being sabath day & hee refused monday til eieninge being a Saints day. I have hiered a house, If I use it, for 16 Xados. I pleaded hard to bee free from all duties telling ye Governer that I tould him soe much before I made my bargain, but hee tould me It could not bee Avoyded. Wherupon I desired to know all Dutys that could bee demaunded, which hee tould me was only this & one per Cent Customs for ye goods into port & ye Murteen out.

20th   I acted noethinge of businesse nither went Ashore it being Sunday, but ye Governer sent me A present of fruite & desired me to visit him to Morrow morninge —

21   I visited ye Governer who bid me not let this businesse trouble me, for since I came hither with his licence hee would see I should not bee injured & bid me visit ye Padry & see what hee said to me, which I did. & the Jesuite would have had me given it under my hand to submit to the determination of two or three knowen men upon their oath before ye Justice, which I refused laying ye businesse wholly on ye Governer, pretending that I could not answer it to have to doe with particuler men in A publick affaire & hee said it noe thinge concerned ye Governer. But I left him & acquainted ye governer ther with who asked me what I said to it, whither I ought to pay it or not. To which I answered I know not & hee tould me it was A thinge disputable amongst many but bid me bee Contented & hee would take up ye matter. This day being A Holiday I could bee permitted to land noethinge. I was like wise informed by Sr Vincente Joan A dew [16] marchant that it is ye opinion of many, yea most, marchants that we ought not to pay this duty.

22th   I visitted ye governer in ye morninge, who tould me hee had sent his Padry to Agitate with ye Jesuit about my businesse & would send me word what I should doe somtime today. & meeting his Padry by ye way, hee tould me what had passed & that ye governer had taken ye businesse upon him selfe. But ye Jesuit would not lett ye staff goe out of his

---

[16] Diu (Dew, Dio, Due), on the tip of Gujarat, west India, is located on the first point of land on the Indian shore as ships return from Persia. Its good and well-protected harbor was important in the sixteenth century, and it received much shipping from the western world and from Malabar.

hands but on tearms which was to have it under his hand & that Instantly such was his, & usualye their Insolencie. Soe ye governer gave me Licence to disinbarq: ye goods when I would but ye day was soe far spent that I could disinbarq noethinge but my Lumber [i.e., miscellaneous stored articles.]

23th I landed A Bale of every sorte that I might have goods to shew such marchants as demaunded them. I presented ye kings ffactor with 4 bottles Sheras [wine] & 40: Rosewater — who: was curteous in expressions & lett us bringe our goods home without takeing any notice of them & trusted to my worde ffor their Contents. But ye basie Jesuit would neds have an Invoyce though hee had noethinge to doe with me but I put him of [f] as farely as I could.

24 The marchants are all agreed for they will not profer soe much as ye Currentt price is by A good Deale & yett at their prices the goodes will yeild Conciderable profitt.

28th I have been informed & have alsoe experimented that ye Portugall marchants of this place use much baffeling dealinge for they have made severall prizes for goods & falen from their worde.

29 The Governer sent for me & siad [*sic*] he was very angry with me for profering to sale those goods hee had bought, meaninge ye Paups. Wherof hee yett wanted 300 corge which I was faine to graunt him at ye former price.

30 Hee sent to me for 400 corge Paups & 40 corge veneas [cloth ornamented with some narrow strips of suitable material], which I could not graunt, but spared him 120 corge Paups. The rest I had promised to some marchants & the Ivory I shall have shortly & way some of it to morrow.

Aug 9 The Governer hath put me off by delays & pretences for payment, but now his Shipp being arrived from Sena [17] hee promises faire. But with out her Arrivall I perceive wee should not bee paid nor have been permitted to depart ffrom hence, for hee would have found pretences to have stayd us,

---

[17] Sena was the principal town of the river district of the Zambezi. In the 1650s it consisted of no more than thirty Portuguese houses and no fort. The Zambezi itself was lined with great estates owned by the Portuguese.

though hee hath much more Ivory in possession then hee oweth us. This morninge ye kings ffactor, comeinge to take our Invoyce, Advised me to bee cautious of stealing custome of [f] goods, accquainting me that it was confiscate if taken. To which I replied that our goods were cource & ye Customs reasonable, 1 per cent, & I would not venture ye Losse & shame for soe smale a matter. But hee tould me I must pay ye Customs of Goa,[18] which was 20 per Cent into Port for our goods & as much out for our Ivory out. Wherat being much amazed & discontented haveing upon ye former demaund for Don de Viages [presumably the merchant represented by the Jesuit priest] desired ye Governer to accquaint me with all duties demaundable, & if I could not submit to pay them to give me leave to quit his Porte. Wherupon hee tould me that noethinge but that & ye Customs of this place 1 per cent in & ditto for Ivory out, soe that I thought of noe more. But ye ffactor seing me discontented tould me that as hee was ye kings Servant it was his Duty to demaund it but bed me have recource to ye Governer about it. Wherupon I visitted ye Governer & accquainted him herewith & hee replyed that he had been preadvised therof & taken Advice there in & ye Goa marchants that were here were our enemies & pleaded that wee ought to pay it but ye Due & Choule marchants not. & hee for his owne parte thought it not fitt but would advise with some marchants that were our ffriends & Conclude ye businesse. & noething but this dubious answer could I gett from him.

11th   At my next vizitt I desired to be resolved about ye Customs, which he tould me should bee noe more than one per Cent as he tould me at first & for our payment hee had not Eliphants teeth to pay, as our bargain was, but could spare us what hee could of that spetie & ye rest in good gold [i.e., fine or pure in quality]. I urged ye payment acording to agreement which would not be graunted, perceiveing which I desired such payment as hee proffered which hee would

---

[18] The customs of Goa were duties levied by the king of Portugal on goods coming in to market and on goods being exported. This was in addition to the customs, mentioned earlier, levied by the Jesuit priest.

not doe pretending many more debts than hee could pay & if he should presently pay me others would exclame upon him. I omitted not daly visiting him & demaunding payment but was still put of[f] which ye Master of ye Ship inputed to be my fault & desired that he might goe with me to ye governer pretending that hee would say much to him, wherfore to satisfie him I took him with me And

17th   We visited him, & ye Customs of Goa being redemaunded by ye ffactor I acquainted him therewith who plainly tould me it was formerly paid by ye ffrancis [19] some 10 years agoe & I must likewise deposit it. But if ye vizroy would gratifie ye President in remitting it, it should be restored, to which purpose I should have A receipt. For ye same urginge our payment I was put of[f] & tould that I must of necesitie stay till hee had dispatched his other businesse. Wherupon I tould him if he dealt soe with us I must protest against him & desired him not to take it ill of me for I was bound to doe it & hee bid me make 20: if I would. And soe wee left him & the Masters great sayings were utered in silence.

19th 20th   I went to ye Castle but was not admited to speak with him.

21   I sent to desire leave to inbarq what I had ashore, which was graunted, & I was tould that to morow night I should be payd.

22   I went for our dispatch & received payment in bad gould [i.e., of defective quality or worth] abateing 450 Xados for duties to ye Capt of these voyages in Goa, which formerly hee tould me hee would take upon his Accountt & gave me A gold Chaine for the President & soe dispatched me.

I would have protested against the Governer for this ill dealing in making us pay Customs of goa when hee had promised the Contrary, for falling from his bargain, for deteining the Ship, & stoping 450 Xados for ye Capt of these voyages in Goa, but could not for want of language wherfore Am forct to bee silent. Now ye reason of his deteining

---

[19] This is a reference to the governor of Daman (Damão) who leased the English pinnace *Francis* from the East India Company in 1640. She loaded goods in Cambay and described them as belonging to the governor of Surat. Shipping was then done under the English flag to avoid seizure by the Dutch.

us soe long was that their Goa & dew Ships might begon before us, for they feared us though they were 4 to sett saile togither.

This place is A barren & unhealthfull place [20] caused by itts barrennesse rather then the Climate & of it selfe affords very little trade, which they manadge by sending their Caferys [21] & sometimes white men to Maccoa [22] some 10 days Journy with smale Quantities at A time of Camikees [23] Paups who: commonly returne them nere duble their value in Ivory which they receive in truck from ye Natives, for their Cloth. The maine nere Adjacent affords much Ebony which they esteeme little of & when any man wants it he may have it for the Charges of fetching which eivry one cannot Doe for want of boats, for I beleive that except ye Governers, there is not 2 boats belonging to ye Island of any capasity for they comonly goe to ye main in Prows [i.e., boats, open decked and lateen rigged] to fetch their provisions of frutie etc. which generally cometh from thence. But nither Maine nor Island affords any flesh or Graine; or yett good water. Without much trouble to fetch it they have good & plenty of Oranges, Lemons, & Cokernutts. Other fruits, hearbs, & Roots they have in their Gardens for their particuler uses but none are sould in ye market. A smale henn will cost 12d & A Loafe of Bread about the weight of A Peny loafe costs 3d. & Beife or Mutton is not procuerable at any rates, nither is fish plentifull. & water for our use we could not procure at all times though we paid 3d for A small pott full which A woman usualy carys on her head. Findeinge these things soe it seemed to me A mistery how they subsisted, but by inquiry I finde they are Cheiflie Supplied with rice & wheat from

---

[20] Mozambique possessed no fresh water and no firewood, and produced few provisions. Either water had to be brought from the mainland or rainwater was used.

[21] "Caffre," a corruption of the Arabic word "kaffir" meaning "unbeliever," was a term used by the Portuguese to designate the Bantu tribe or Negroes in general.

[22] Mocha (Maccoa) is a small seaport in southwest Arabia, on the Red Sea.

[23] Cannequin (Cannikeen), a white cotton cloth from east India, was folded in a square manner and usually 8 ells (10 yards) in length.

Goa & Likewise Conserias which is ye Cheife diet of ye Better sorte. Some rice, ambergreece, & Sheepe they have from Masseluge [24] & assada where beius [i.e., beefs] are very plentifull, but they will not bestow ye salting it. Some rice, etc., they have from Sena & more might have by relation if they would take the pains. Of this place [i.e., Sena] I heare A very good report. It leyith in A river in somewhat lesse than 20 degrees, whence cometh all their Gould and thereof is good Quantities, comeing from 2 severall mines [25] upon that river, which is all ye mines I can heare of upon this Coast. Ye Cheife & all most only comodity for this place & all ye Coast is Cannikeens Paups. Ye next is veineas, wherof 1 1/10 [i.e., one-tenth] parte (will not vend) soe much as paups. Some Course Byrams Selaes & Guzze Baftas [26] will Likewise vend, but in very small Quantities & likewise some Cource Brawles; but fine goods are All to gither impropper here. Sena doth vend about 600 tunns [large casks, in this case used as a measure of capacity for cargo] of these sorts of goods in A year & their returnes are in Gould & som Ivory & slaves as many as they will & Cheap for ye value of A Ryall of 8/8 [i.e., rial of eight or pieces of eight, the Spanish "dollar"]. They reporte that some Portugalls that reside there kepe upwards of A thousand slaves, and few that are there that have not hundreds which they inploy in transportation of their goods. They have noe fortification there, only severall places of residence situated upon ye river. & ye Governers ffactory is at ye enterance of ye river where the Ships usually ride. Noe Shipp can goe thither of ye Portugalls without compounding with ye Governer of Mosambiq which usually they doe for ⅓ parte of ye goods. The People are very Peaceable & doubtlesse it is A very brave trade that they have thither. I doe

---

[24] Masseluge is an island off the west coast of Madagascar, about one and a half miles in length. The eastern end has a bay with a good harbor for wintering. The nearby mainland has good provisions.

[25] Sofala (see footnote 27) had the richest gold mines in the area. Manica and Mashona were the principal gold fields.

[26] The first was some sort of coarse cloth. Guzzy was a very poor kind of cotton cloth. "Baftas" or "baffetas" is derived from a word meaning "woven." This cloth was about 12½ yards in length and 1 yard wide; the best examples of it came from Surat.

probablie computate that they bring thence yearly upwards of 20000 oz. gould And that Mosambige & ye places thereto subordinate afford yearly nere 100 tunn of Eliphants teeth.

The next place considerable to this is Cofalla, an Island leying in about 20½ degrees whence they have A good trade to ye Adjacent maine for Ivory & Amber greece, but noe great Quantities of either. The island is fortified with A Castle but I beleive very weakly maned.[27]

ffurther thay have A trade to Ingumbane,[28] a place betwixt Sofalla & Cape Corintas & likewise at Cape Corintas & further in A large Bay [i.e., Delagoa Bay] in 26 degrees So. lattitude, to which places they doe not yearly voyage but sometimes once in two, sometimes once in 3 years. Whence I have been informed they have brought 120 Bahars of Ivory 40 or 50 Ruttles of Amber greece besides Seahorse teeth [i.e., hippopotamus teeth, a form of ivory] etc. The Comodities vendable in those places are the prementioned Cloathinge, alsoe Pautcas or Cource Dutties,[29] smale beads of all Collours, 4 or 500 Mamudis[30] Surratt [and] ould Copper or Brasse which hath been used in Potts etc. & broken to pieces wherof they make Shackles [i.e., ornaments such as an armlet or anklet]. Directions for the Roads latitudes or harboure of ye 2 prementioned places I could gett none but in ye No. part of Bay [i.e., Delagoa Bay] there is A large River [Rio Incomati]

---

[27] Cofalla, i.e., Sofala (Soffalla) is located at the mouth of the river Sofala, 400 miles southwest of Mozambique. It was an ancient Arab and early Portuguese port important for gold and iron. The fort at Sofala was in disrepair. In 1635 orders were issued to have it refortified to hold a garrison of 200. Later, in 1652, the governor of Mozambique arrived there with orders to tear down the fort, since it was thought to be unnecessary, but he decided to leave it standing in the interest of Portuguese prestige and for the defense of the few local residents.

[28] Inhambane (Ingombane) was a seaport just north of Cape Corintas on Inhambane Bay, an inlet of the Mozambique Channel. There was no port at Cape Corintas.

[29] Indian cotton cloths, called pautkas, were white, brown or blue, and usually of a particular length and width. The "cource dutties" were coarse cotton cloths woven in Surat. The name comes from the Hindu word "dhoti" or "dhoty" which is a loincloth worn by the Hindu castes of upper India.

[30] The mamudi (Ma., Mds., Ms.), a coin of India and Gujarat, was valued at about 12d.

wherin is a brave Island [31] of 8 or 10 Leagues longe to ye Westward wherof the Shipps Ride in 7 ffathoms water close to ye Shore from whence they trade up ye River in their boats & likewise to other Rivers in ye same bay wherof there are 3 or 4 besides this [the other rivers entering the bay are the Matola, the Tembe, and the Maputa].

29th Wee passed by ye Island Momfiar [32] which we toke to be Zenzebar it being falce laid downe in our platts [i.e., maps or charts]. I cannot well judg of ye Largnesse of ye Island but it showeth little to ye Eastward.

30th We saw Zanzabar which we took to be Pemba. We sailed by it all day with a fresh gaile & in ye Eiveninge we discovered a bay [probably the channel between the island of Tumbatu and Zanzibar itself at the north end of Zanzibar] wherin is good Anchoring Latt. 5:55 No. into which we gott about sunn sett. Next morning sent ye boats ashore unto severall places but ye People left their habitations & would not bee spoken with. After dinner I went in ye Long boat & hapilie we espied a boat which we fetched up & spake with ye People who tould us that ye Island was Zanzabar belonging to ye King of Portugall & in ye Place was noe trade but if we would goe to ye part of ye Island where ye Portugalls inhabited they would Pilot us. Demaundinge whither they would give us A Pilott for Pemba were deneyed sayinge they darst not, because the Portugalls had wars with that kinge.[33]

31th In ye Eivening wee sett saile having given ye man of ye Island a Ryall 8/8 & lett him goe who tould us wee should Discover Pemba in 3 howers saile. This island of Zanzabar is up wards of 20 Leagues longe.

m
7:br In ye Morning early we discover Pemba fare by though we lay A try [i.e., spread the sail in order to keep the ship

---

[31] Chefina Grande was the largest of three islands which also included Chefina Pequena and Chefina do Meio.
[32] Monfia or Mafia Island is located off the coast of Africa, just south of Zanzibar. It has an area of 200 square miles.
[33] During the period 1651–1652, the governor of Mombasa put down a rebellion at Zanzibar and also fought against the returning ships of the king of Pemba, capturing five and driving the crews of the others ashore to fight. Pemba was kept under submission as an important source of provisions for Mombasa.

1   more steady and turn her bow toward the direction of the wind] all night yett ye Currentt [34] sett us to the No. beyond expectation, & we went to ye Westward of it being informed ye harbor was there & came to an Anchor under An Island [probably Makongwe, which lies just off the coast near Mkoani] some ffive Leagues within ye Island where we happened upon A towne called Muckoanne [i.e., Mkoani] where ye People seemed joyfull of our comeing, but darst nither give or sell us anythinge in leau without order from ye king, but tould me if I would send a Letter to ye king I should have an answer of it to morrow & might be supplied with what we desired.

2d   I wrote to ye kinge & ye 3d had an answer & libertie to com to Court. & his slaves had order to furnish us with what soever provisions we wanted that ye Island afforded upon his accountt & to take noething for it & they furnished us with A Bullock & great plenty of fruite. But being informed by ye People that it was 10 or 15 Leagues to ye kings towne I could not undertake such A Journey afoote wherof I bad them advise ye king & desire him to send A Pilot to carry ye Ship nerer to his towne or to pilot our boate to some place nere him or to inorder some other transport for me.

4   The 4th came downe A Pilott but to noe purpose for hee would not carry us to a place any nerer than wee were & the king had inordered Slaves to carry me supposeinge I had a Pallinkeene [i.e., palanquin]. But time spending soe fast & this being A this being A [sic] businesse not to be effected without ye Losse of 8 or 10 days, I resolved to haste away for Pate.[35] Wherfore ye 5th I sent ye kinge A present & expresed my not coming, promising by gods helpe to vizitt him ye

---

[34] This current, referred to several times by Buckeridge, is a treacherous one, sweeping northward through the Mozambique Channel and flowing on the east side of the Zanzibar and Pemba channels. During the southwest monsoon, the speed of the current is about two to four miles per hour, during the northeast monsoon about one to three miles per hour.

[35] Pate (Patta) is a small island 15 miles long and at its widest part 7 miles; at this time it had three prosperous towns.

next year but desired him to graunt leave to his People to sell us 2 or 3 Cattle for we intended to stay 1 or 2 days.

6 [36] The 6th came A Letter from ye kinge adviseing that his procuradore was comeing with what things wee wanted & should advise me with what things he wanted against next year. Hee arriveing brought A present from ye kinge: Vizt:

    4: Bulloks
    4: ffardles [bundles or small packets] Rice
    4: Potts Butter

ffruite in Abundance, milke, henns, & such like what could
7 [37] be procured. Soe because I would not be ungratefull I sent ye kinge A 2d present. And the 7th we left ye shore with intent to sett saile that eivning but could not.

The 8th we set saile for Pate but could not com to sight of it which I rather Impute to ye Masters over timorousness in keping from sight of ye Shore till the Currentt sett us beyond it, then to anyother valued reason hee had for it.

11th We saileing A long ye Shore had sight of A towne in ye latitude of Brava [38] about 1: degre No. Being noe roade to appearence wherfore I desired that ye boat might be sent A shore, alledging that though it seemd & they pretended it Dangerous for ye Shipp to goe nere the Shore yett Questionlesse ye boat might secuerly goe. To which I could have noe answer till it was to late & then many more then convenient. & ye boat was goeing to bee hoisted out but it was to late for we had over shot ye place, & imediatly mad another towne larger than that but noe harbor to appearence. Wherefore it being evieninge & beinge to deale with an obstenate disposition we sailed by it in silence, veiuing A very faire City & 4: large Musseets [a kind of ship] & 2: vessells not Certain whither afloat or not.

---

[36] 5 has been crossed out.
[37] 6 has been crossed out.
[38] Brava (Braba) is a coast town, about 100 miles southwest of Magadoxa (Mogadishu).

II

The following short account seems to be the only surviving record of a voyage of one Michael Ashmore to Mombasa in 1647. Neither he nor his ship, the *Successe*, was located in the India House Original Correspondence files for that period or in the Court Minutes. The brief notations transcribed here no doubt were used as sailing directions for such relatively unknown ports along the coast of Africa as Malindi and Sofala.

Abstracted from A Journall of Mr. Michaell Ashmors made in Ship Successe of Damon to Mombas:[1] 1647

ffebr 20th Lattitude by observation [i.e., determined by measuring the altitude of the sun] at noone degrees: 3:58 M North. At :6: houers [in the] eivening saw land on the Main, on ye Cost of Abex.[2] Winds from ENE to NE:b:E cource

    WSW: 66:2 —
    WBS: 49:3 —

21: Stered along ye Shore some: 24 miles of winds from ENE: to ESE: courc: W   9 —
    stream helped in 2 days   WBS   21 —
    80 Miles WSW   SW:BW: 54 —
    SW BS   8 —

This eivening saw Magadoxo [Mogadishu, Mogadiscio] bearing WNW 6 leags of[f] ye towne, laying in A smale Bay with a low white poynt to ye NE & bE, ye land being not very high over it & not remarkable. Hee that is bound

---

[1] Mombasa (Mombass, Bombas, Bombasse, Mombasse) is an island located 150 miles north of Zanzibar at the mouth of a deep bay. It was probably settled by the Arabs in the eleventh century. Vasco da Gama arrived there in 1498; from 1529 to 1698 it was held by the Portuguese.

[2] The coast of Mozambique to the Red Sea is commonly called the coast of Abex. The Portuguese referred to it as the coast of Malindi.

for this towne must keepe ye shore Closse abord [i.e., keep close to the shore] or hee wilbe putt by with ye Stream [i.e., caught in the current]. Latt: d:2:21 No. and Meridean:23:07. Hee found himselfe 2 degrees more westerly than by accountt & alloued him selfe in degrees:25:07 west from St. Johns.³

22   Latt de:0:58 Minuts No. Meridean W:26:55 the Stream: SW:B.W: helped 60 miles, winds from S:B.E to SE: 8 Lea-[gues] from Shore cource: NW:b:W: 06:3 —
                                              W: 12:0 —
                                        W:BS. —   32:6 —
                                        SWBW: 12:6 —
                                        SSW —   20:0 —

22:   This eviening ye towne of Braba bore from us NW distance 15 Miles. Some 8 Leagus to ye no. east & B:eest of this towne yow shall see A white sandy Bank in ye land up to ye very top of the land. & before yow come to ye towne yow shall see 3 more distance one from ye other some 7 Miles. & after yow have passed to ye westward yow shall see 3 more which is ye most remarkable Land of all the land he saw —

23   Latt:29 Minuts South Merid: des: 28:46: West Winds from: ESE to SEbS: Cource: WSW:14:0 —
        Stream: WSW 69 miles —   SWbW:33:5 —
                                      SWbS:27:5 —
When yow are thwart of Hugos, which leys under ye line, yow⁴ shall see great groves of trees & will continew soe some 10 Leagus. & then ye land doth rise in little humaks like smale Islands all the way betwene this & the towne of Pate.

24:   Latt:1:28:So: Merid: W:30:01: winds from SSE to SEbE: cource   SWbS: 22:00
                                      SW — 28:00 }58:=
        Stream: 59 Miles   ENE — 8:00

5 Leagus from shore all this Land som 20 Leagus to the NE

❦❦❦❦❦❦❦❦❦❦❦❦❦❦❦❦❦

³ Probably Juan de Nova, which was used as a navigation aid in the passage through the Mozambique Channel. The island was named after the Portuguese captain who discovered it in 1501.
⁴ The reference is to the Iungo River, which lies just north of the equator, here mistakenly referred to as being under the equator.

& bE of ye Island Pata is all smale Islands⁵ & ye main not to be seene. Hee saw 3 Shipps that bore into ye Shore & Anchored.

25   Latt: 2:09 So: Merid: 30:16: W: wind from S: to SE =
                                          Cource   SSE: 16: —
         Stream: 14 Miles-W:S:W: SW: 14 —
                                           SWBS: 32 —

26:   Latt by Judgmt 1:54 So: Merid: 30:06: W calme but Ship drove as aserved by bearings of Land NEbN:18 miles. They saw 3 smale vessells —

27:   Latt by observation not very good 1:45: South nerid [meridian] dist[ant] 29:57: W winds: SE & SEbE steme: SSW & SWbS: 20 miles but by ye bearings of ye land drove NEbN: 12 miles. At 2 houers [in the] afternoone ye Island Pate bore NW some 8 miles of[f]. Bore up to Anchor without ye Bar of Ampasa [i.e., outside the shoal or bank of sand between the town of Ampasa or Faza and the channel to the mainland] 9 howers after noone in: 15 ffatham water, gray sandy ground & had ye land on these bareings. Ye SE Poynt of ye Island Burgone bore NE ½ No. dist 8 miles. Ye Bar of Ampasa: NW:som:7 miles dist. Ye So. E: poynt of ye Island Pata W ½ N: dist 9 miles. From ye Poynt leys A ledg of rocks 2 miles, with poynt of ye ledg bore WbS. I Judg ye Island Pate to lay in latt:ld40m So. Merid wt from St John — d: 30:04 W ye Island Pata is som 3 Leagus long & hath 3 Arabs towns⁶ on it. It is ye Cheif place of trade of these parts. 6 leagus to ye NE of this Island yow shall see A square Patch of land like A table. & some 2 leagus to ye W yow shall rais ye Island burgone in smale humacks & A white patch of Land which is ye most remarkable part to finde this Island. About d:3:06 M So. leys A ledg [of] Rocks off of ye towne of Melinde⁷ except which is noe danger to Mombas which is

---

⁵ From the island of Pate northeast along the coast of the mainland some twenty leagues, the continental shelf is very wide with many shoals, rocks, and islands.

⁶ The three prosperous towns were Pate, on the southeastern part of the island, Siyu on the west, and Faza, or Ampasa, on the north end. The latter became the strongest supporter of the Portuguese on the African coast.

⁷ Malindi was a seaport town visited in 1498 by Vasco da Gama, who

an Island invironed by ye main in A small Bay scarce desernable at Sea byt [but] by 3 hills called 3 Brothers. [i.e., the port would have been difficult to recognize from the sea except for three hills lying north of the town] Som ½ A league to ye No: of Bombas, ye 2 poynts Land that make ye Bay are foull with Ledges of Rocks desernable by Breaches at high water by appearance. At low therare 2 harbors land locked ffortified with A Castle & 14:Gunns 40 Souldiers & not above 100 other Portugalls. Lat:4:00 So. Merid W:31: 40: — On ye Ledges yow may borrow to 4 ffatham ye No. Ledg.

---

erected a monument which is still standing. Its important products were gold and ivory.

III

This undated list of accounts is not in Buckeridge's handwriting. The Mr. Massee listed could be either Jonathan Massey or Walter Massey, both of whom were employed as factors at Bantam at this time. Mr. James Bostock was also on Company service there, and was later sent to the Banda Islands. Mr. William Gurney was a factor in Bengal, Masulipatam, and Fort St. George, where he died September 7, 1653. The ship *Hinde* carried trade goods between Surat and Bantam, and also to Basra and Madras. She is described as having very low decks, no accommodations for passengers, and a capacity of about 300 tons. William Nokes, servant to the president of the Surat factory of the East India Company, returned to England in 1654. Tulsi Das Khan Parak, referred to here as Tulcidas Parrat, was for many years a banker or money changer. He was described as "a very honest and industrious man and deserves substantial incouragement" (O.C. 2204).

Remembr to demaund an Accountt of Mr. Bostock & Mr. Massee of goods sent from Suratt to Bantam to Mr. Gurny by Ship Hinde ffrom Mr. Wm. Nokes belonging to —
Tulcidas Parrat Vizt marked as in margent [the initials TP appear in the lefthand margin of this page]
1 Ba[le] Sorts vizt No 1
  Baftas Blew 9 corge at 70 Ma [mahmudis]:   630:00
  Satt Blew [true satin made from silk]
    5 corge at 40 ":"   200:00
1 Ba[le] No 5 [containing?] vizt:
  Baftas broad [1]: 23 guz: 2:17 at 150 Ma: 427:16
  Bafta: broach [2] fine: 3¼ corge cost Ma: 1276:16
  Byrams blew: corge 2:6 peeces cost   92:00

---

[1] A kind of coarse and cheap fabric, generally cotton. In this case, wide pieces of the cloth.

[2] Broach is located on the Narbada River about 30 miles from the Gulf of Cambay. For centuries it was an important travel and trade center and famed for its fabrics. The English factory there was established in 1616.

Chints Amada[3]: 5:10 cost	236:08
Tapwhindas[4] 4 double peeces	8:00
1 Ba[le] No: [containing?] vizt:	
Brawles Jota[5] 12½ corge cost	375:00
Chints Amada: 3: ¾ cost	187:16
Baftas blew: 2:07 cost	143:16
1 Ba[le] of Ramgee Mettas:	
Baftas broad 2 corge	400:00
Salloos: 15 peeces	33:24
	4010:00
Charges	200:00
	4210:00

Herof were sould by Mr. Gurney & carryed to ye Coast ye proceed

Baftas ffine	3:05 peeces ffor Rys [reis]	341:00
Baftas Blew	2:00	104:—
Byrams	2:06	28:—
		472: [473]

---

[3] Painted or stained calicoes imported from Ahmadabad, the capital of the province of Gujarat or Cambay.
[4] Tappichindaes, a cotton cloth.
[5] A blue and white striped cloth, sometimes called turban, because it was used to cover the head, particularly on the coast of Africa.

IV

This entry is a puzzling one. It seems to be a copy of a report or letter to the president or Company concerning Buckeridge's second African trip. A general description of each port is given, together with details on the best goods to be sold there and other information as well. The report is dated July 15, 1663, some ten years after the second voyage as here recorded. These pages seem to be in the same hand as the preceding goods list, but it is signed with the initials N.B. In the original the letter is divided into two parts, the final three pages appearing much later in the manuscript. The text is presented here in one undivided section. The question of why the letter precedes material of an earlier date has not been answered.

Worshipfull Sir

    According to your order, I shall here give you ye best Relacion I can of what Ports are traded unto & what trade is accustomarilie used in them by ye Portugalls on ye Coasts of Soffalla & Melinde.
    Begining with A Bay to ye Southward of Cape Corintas [Delagoa Bay] in som what above 25½ degrees So: latitude, whither ye Governer of Mosambiq doth usualie send A Shipe once in two or three years of about 100 tunns burthen, Laden cheifelie with A sort of short narrow cource blew callicoes & for Sortments [a varied collection of goods and articles used for trade] some smale quantities of finer Blew red white & checkered callicoes & about 2 tunns of Cource glasse beads that are procurable cheap in Indea. I doe not beleive ye Cargo doth cost in Indea above [crossed out: 600] 800 lb & doth produce 4 or 5 [changed from 3 or 4] thimes as much at ye least [undeciphered marginal additions to this line crossed out]. As it is now managed by ye Captain or Governer of Mosambiq who alone injoys ye trade & probablie if any of an other nacion were competitor with him in this trade it would not bee soe advantagious to nither as it now is to him. At this place ye Portugalls are nither fortified nor have they either Plantacion or factory, but only voyage as affore said once in 3 years. Ye returns are cheiflie made in Ivory & Amber grece, ye first 90 Bahars, ye latter 2 or 300 ozs.

The next port is Ingombanee in about 21: degrees So: Latitude, traded to yearlie by ye Governer of Mosambiq who hath ye sole trade of ye place, with A Ship about 100 tunns burden & A cargo much like ye premencioned, which usualy maks him A very good returne, cheiflie Ivory about 50 or 60 Bahars yearlie & 100 oz: amber grece though not altogither soe good as that to cape corintas, it being ffrequented but once in 2 or 3 years. At this place is nither ffort, Planctacon, nor ffactory of ye Portugalls.

Soffalla, antiently ye most famous, & giveing name to ye whole coast, is an Island ffortified & peopled by thee Portugalls though the ffort almost totalie ruined, as I was informed. And ye trade [crossed out: almost totalie] in a manner quite diverted to Sena whence, or rather from Chelimana,[1] whence it is Supplyed by smale vessells with that little goods it vends with ye Captain of Mosambiq accountt & whither they usualie make returns therof in Eliphants Teeth.

Sena is A River leying in nerest : 18: degrees So. Lattitude: where ye Captain or Governer of Mosambiq: hath A ffactory caled Chelemana about 12 Miles from ye river Mouth, & there constantlie resides 10 or 15 ffamelies of Portugalls & Mustefas [half-caste, probably Portuguese-African] to take care of ye goods & send them up in flatt bottomed boats to ye toune or Cittie of Sena, reported to be rich & populous of Portugalls & mustefas which is said to bee above 40 Leagus up ye river. & they are usualie 12 or 15 days goeing thither with their Loaden boats. Thence they are caried up ye countrey to ye mines on mens backs. Hither ye Captain or Governer of Mosambiq sends yearlie 3 or 4: Shipps from one to 200 Tunns burthen: laden with very little other goods than that sort of coure blew callicoes fformerly spoken of & hath his returnes cheiflie in sand Gould [gold dust], wherof I doe beleive ye place produces yearly about 20000: ozs. Some Eliphants Teeth it doth alsoe afford but noe great quantitie. Betwene this & Mosambq are some smale Ports traded to only by boats of litle Importance.

Mosambiq an Islan in nerest 15 degrees south latitude [is] A Barren & unhealthy place not affording of it selfe soe much as good water for ye inhabitants, but very comodeous for A large & safe harbour Secured & fortified with A strong Castle, ye toune being well built &

---

[1] Quelimane (Chelemana) is a small seaport town about twelve miles inland from the mouth of the Quelimane River, in the Zambezi River system. The town became notorious for its exportation of slaves.

peopled with Portugall & mustefas, able to resist A conciderable enemie. Ye inhabitants of Mosambiq have free libertie to trade up into ye countrey nere Mosambq for Ivory & provisions & alsoe in smale vessails to some pettie ports & Islands betwene Mosambiq & Quiloa [2] as alsoe to Masselage, Assada [and] Joanna [3] &c., but not at all to ye southward of Mosambiq except it bee once in 3 years to Sena wher they pay ye Captain or Governer [crossed out: 30 per cent for] a third part of what they cary thither for libertie. Ye Portugalls doe Trade to Mosambiq from Goa, Choule, & Dio with 7 or 8 Shipps A year of about 2 or 300 Tunns burthen, and Mosambiq, with ye places Subordinate thereto, doth yearly produce about 100 Tunns of Eliphants Teeth & ye quantitie of Gould formerly spoken of ffrom Sena.

Quiloa, ye ffirst Port on ye Coast of Melinde, is on An Island in A large bay a little under 9 degrees So. lattitude. It is only traded unto by ye Governer of Mombass & such as hee gives leave to & vends cheiflie that sort of cource blew callicoe that vends at Mosambiq & ye Coast of Soffalla. There doth alsoe vend divers sorts of Cambona [4] checkquered Callicoes as Brawles Longues, &c. & some of ye ordenary sort of: Red, blew, white, & Browne Callicoes. Also Iron vends well in ye place but I beleive noe great quantitie. Ye principall comodities that it affords are Eliphants Teeth, Bees Wax, & tortice Shells; [5] but of ye last A Smale quantitie.

Zinzibar [6] is an Island ye Southernmost end of it Leying in nerest 6: 20 M So. lattitude. The Toune or place of Trade leying about ye midle of ye Island on ye West side of it. Ye navigacion to it is dangerous, but from Quiloa you may have Pilots. Ye trade is much like that at Quiloa but ye greatest part of their Trade is brought from ye

---

[2] This island and bay is about 400 miles north of Mozambique. Once in the possession of the Portuguese, it was given up by them because of the serious illnesses contracted by the inhabitants. Its port carried on an extensive trade with Sofala.

[3] Johanna (Joh:, Johana), a port in the Comoro Islands just northwest from Madagascar. There was a good bay, with excellent provisions, wood, and water.

[4] Cambay, at the end of the Gulf of Cambay, was one of India's most important seaports. It was famous for calicoes and precious stones.

[5] The shells of certain tortoises, especially that of the hawk's-bill turtle, *Chelone imbricata*, is semitransparent with a mottled or clouded coloration, and is used extensively in ornamental work such as inlay.

[6] Zanzibar (Zanquebar) was a seaport of early importance to Portuguese settlement on the East African coast. It is 53 miles long, 24 miles across at its widest point, with an area of 640 square miles.

Maine land which is in sight of ye Island it affording little it selfe & that of such sorts as procurable at Qiloa.

Pemba [7] is an Island leying in about 5 ½ degrees So. lattitude but affords of it selfe little but bees wax & provisions, unlesse they have Peace with ye Portugalls that they may trade to ye maine, which they had not when I was there nor nere 10 years before. But all these places were nere ruined by warrs with ye Portugalls which they doe cheiflie manage by devideing these Petty Princes & Governers & imploying their forces against one an other. Nor doe the Portugalls suffer any they can hinder to trade to any of these places espetialie ye Arabians & Indeans whom they doe punish with Confiscacion of vesaile & goods (if not captivitie of their persons) if they are taken tradeing there.

Mombass is ye Principall place on this coast; though it be called ye Coast of Melinde takeing its name from ye towne of Melinde that leys betwene Mombasse & Pate, A place of little moment at present; [Mombasa] being reported to bee An Island well fortified [8] by ye portugalls & hath A very convenient harbour whither Annualie doth come from Indea: 7 or 8: Shipps about 2 or 300 Tunns burthen. & after they have there unladen part of theire goods 4 or 5 [changed from 3 or 4] of them doe usualie goe to Pate with good part of their Cargo, where they ffind vent for it.

Pate is an Island nere ye equinoctiall Line which hath Safe harbours but dangerous to bee com to: inhabited by Arrabbans & other Mahometans. But ye Portugalls have ye cheife trade there & did take customs of all others that did trade thither. & ffrom Mombasse & this place they did usualie carie to Indea A greater quantitie of Eliphants Teeth then they doe from Mosambiq, besides A good quantitie of Bees Wax & Tortice Shells, some Civett [9] & ambergreece also procurable here. Ye goods that vend here are Cheiflie callicoes, but of A Different & finer sort than at either Mombass or Mosambiq. Alsoe Iron,

---

[7] The island of Pemba has an area of about 380 square miles and is about 30 miles north-northeast of Zanzibar.

[8] The construction of Fort Jesus was begun in 1593, and it is presently considered to be the outstanding historical monument on the Swahili coast. Its normal garrison was 100 men. The chief architect of India, Joao Batista Cairato (actually an Italian military architect Giovanni Batista Cairati), designed it. The fort was finished in the seventeenth century and has not suffered any structural changes since that time.

[9] Civet is a yellowish or brownish substance, having a strong musky smell, obtained from the glands of several animals of the Civet genus, especially of the African civet cat. It is used in perfumery.

cloth, Lead &c. will vend more here than at any other place on these Coasts. These people have A trade to Masselage & Assada on ye Island of St. Lawrence [another name for Madagascar] cheiflie for slaves [crossed out: & cattell &] but some sugar & provisions they have from Assada, but noe great quantitie. But of Slaves they yearly bring from [crossed out: thence] Masselage about 2000 head & Slaves are Cheap & plentifullie to be had at all places on those Coasts but where ye Portugalls came. Comodities they doe not suffer Mahometans to trade espetialie in slaves. Ye Portugalls had A ffactorie fformerly at Ampasa A Toune on ye Island of Pate where they had A Church & Preists & severall families resided there which I saw anno 1653 but in anno 1660 ye Arabbs of Muscatt were there with A fleete & destroyed or captivated all they found there & tooke 6 Saile of Shipps from them that usualie traded betwene Indea & those parts. & what alteracion hath been thereby occasioned since I know not.

Morca [Merca], Braba, & Magadoxa are 3 Townes within 4 degrees to ye No. of the quinoctial line inhabited by Arabbs that have been long free from any Tribute to ye Portugalls. Ye Ports are dificult and dangerous to bee come to though safe when within them. They are yearly traded to with 4 or 5 Tourins, or smale vesails from Suratt, which bring thence A good quantitie of such goods as are usualie brought from Mombasse & Pate. But all that coast from 4 degrees No. lattitude to ye redd Sea doth not afford any place of trade but is for ye most part Shoule & not safe to bee navigated nere ye Shore.

If I have been to breife & not fully expressed what [is] needfull for your informacion, I shall at any time await on yow to give yow ffurther Sattisfaction. In ye mean time humblie rest your obliged ffriend & Servant

July ye 15th anno 1663   N: B:

V

After returning from the trip to Africa, the *Assada Merchant* was next freighted down the coast from Surat to Batticaloa for betel nuts, used by the Europeans as trade goods. She sailed in October 1651. Since there is no report or letter in the manuscript, Buckeridge evidently had no part in this endeavor and was probably employed at Surat on Company business. The ship returned to Surat on January 6, 1652. It was intended that she should next sail to Gombroon and then at the end of March "at hir returne, [she] shalbe employed with a Cargo of goods to ye Coast of Melinda or Ethiophia whither she was sent ye last yeare" (O.C. 2285). After this trip to Persia she was considered in such bad condition that her next trip to Mozambique and other ports was postponed so that she could be repaired. It was too early in the season to send her to Africa, so she made another voyage to Gombroon. Document O.C. 2299 is a copy of the orders to Jeremy Raymond, master of the *Assada Merchant* for the second voyage, titled "Commissions & Instructions Given by us ye President and Councell of India Persia Etc. unto Mr Jeremy Rayman Master of Pinnace Assada Merchant bound from ye Road, unto Cape Corinthes Coast of Soffola, Mussambique Melinde & soe back unto Swally Road whether the Almighty Conduct him." This commission was dated December 12, 1652, at "Swally Mareen" and signed by Jeremy Blackman, Edward Pearce, George Oxinden, and Thomas Bretton. Raymond's orders enjoined him to follow any directions given by Buckeridge: "we desire you to ffollow ye order & direction of ye said Mr Buckeredge to what ports you shall sale, & not to depart thence till he shall order the same likewise, & always to be ayding & assisting him with boates & men in lading and unlading your said Ship & in what elce he shall desire . . ." (See Appendix B for a full transcription of this document.)

A Bodleian manuscript, item reference number Manuscript English History c. 63, a portion of which is printed here as Appendix A, contains the instructions to Buckeridge for this voyage: "Commission & Instructions given by us the President and Councell of India, Persia, Etc unto Mr. Nico. Buckeridg, bound to Cape Corinthes: Coast of Suffola, Mozambiq and Millinda." This commission was also dated December 12, 1652, and signed as above. The following letter, dated December 22, 1652, was written by Buckeridge to the master, Jeremy Raymond, shortly after they embarked upon their voyage to East Africa.

Respected ffriend Mr. Jeremy Raymond

    The President & Councell haveing in their Comition refered yow to my directions for which Parts & places yow shall goe to in this our intended voyage, haveinge had Conference with yow about this matter, wee both agreeing in one opinion upon serious & mature Consideracon I doe upon your request for your Securitie in case of my mortalitie give yow these my desirs in writinge soe timely that yow may conveniently apply your selfe to effect them which are that yow endeavour to make ye Coast of Melinde in nere 4 degrees North Latitude & saile alongst that Shore, that we may discover ye two Townes wee Saw last voyage but could not stop at and soe for the Island of Pate which is one of [the] most Principall Ports upon that Coast & where I hope to finde best Trade & usage. Whence I hope by gods assistance to sett saile for Cape Corintas in ye begining of ffebr or by ye midle at ffurthest, takeing Augustine Bay [1] in our way. This I esteeme ye hopefullest way to make our voyage profitable & to comply with ye President & Councells desires for discovery, to which I desire gods Blessing & Subscribe my selfe.

                                                  Your very Loving ffriend

Pinnace Assada Marchant at Sea   Nicho: Buckeridge
ye 22th Decembr 1652

---

[1] Augustine Bay is on the west coast of Madagascar directly across the Mozambique Channel from Cape Corintas. The English considered the bay very much like that at Dartmouth in England. It was a favorite stopping place for provisions and for resting on the voyage to or from India.

VI

Two brief manuscript pages report the beginning of Buckeridge's second voyage to Africa.

Worthy & Respected ffriends

That yow may the more fully be acquainted by what Conveyance ye inclosed letter came hither, I have framed these lines to advise yow that ye 13 ulto: ffebr [i.e., December 13] Pinnace Assada Marchant sett saile ffrom Swally hole, sent by ye President & Councell to make A discovery on ye Coasts of Melinde & Sofalla in whome hee alsoe sends A letter for ye Comaunders of ye Shipps expected from England hither this year wherof ye inclosed is A Copie, ye originall I cary with me intending god willinge to leave it at Augustine Bay at my comeing there after we have been at Sena, Sofalla, Cape Corintas etc., Ports on that Coast whither by gods permission wee are now bound. We have alreadie been on ye Coast of Melinde And were intended for Pate but ye winds blew soe voyolently & ye Current set soe stronglie that we over shot it soe we made for this place [i.e., Johanna], Purposely to leave these letters, that we may not bee forced to stay here till ye usuall time of ye Suratt Shipps Arivall hither when it will bee to late for us to goe to Pate whither god willing wee intend to be goeing some time in June & to take A Pilot from hence. Wherefore wee intreate yow Our friends intended for ye Coast Cormandell [1] to leave us advice how ye general affairs of England Stand: and whither wee have warr or Peace with holland & Portugall or either of them that wee may regulate ourselvs accordingly. Alsoe pray accquaint us what Shipps & Comaunders are intended from England to Indea this year. I have yett A ffurther request to yow that yow would leave us A Cable & Anchor if yow can possible spare it, ye cable about 11 or 12 Incher,

---

[1] The lower east coast of India roughly from Negapatam to the important port of Masulipatam. The coast has few good harbors and a low shoreline, and is beaten by heavy seas throughout the year, especially during the northeast monsoons from October to April.

the Anchor about 7 or 8 hundred weight.² Wee are in great want herof for wee have been at ye Island of Comra [Comora, at the northern entrance to Mozambique Channel], where we had fair trade & Quarter with ye People, but have lost our best Cable & Anchor & are badly furnished with those Speties & Shall have great ocasion for them when we returne for ye Coast of melinde. The Smirna Marchant ³ was nere halfe laden when we left Swally hole & I hope will sett saile for england before ye Midle of Jainiuary. Ye love ⁴ was safely arived to ye Coast & soe was President Baker from Bantam in ye Roe Buck; but his wife died by ye way, which is All the news I know worth your notice.⁵ So with my Respecitived salutes tendered to your Acceptance I Reddylie Subscribe.

your very Loveing ffreinds

---

² The cable was generally formed of three ropes twisted together, called strands. All ships were to have three good cables — the sheet cable and two bower cables, and all were to be 120 fathoms in length. An eleven incher would have 598 threads and weigh 2392 pounds; the twelve incher 699 threads and weigh 2796 pounds. The anchor was to be seven or eight hundredweight. A hundredweight in the British system is equal to 112 pounds, probably originally equal to 100 pounds.

³ This ship of the East India Company apparently set sail for England on January 10, 1653; it arrived at Falmouth July 3, 1653. It returned to England with more private trade goods aboard than any previous ship. On another trip, in 1660, it was wrecked on the island of Juan de Nova, off the west coast of Madagascar, on its return voyage.

⁴ The ship *Love* was probably about 400 to 450 tons. It was used on the India–England route, carrying such cargo as indigo, piece goods, cinnamon, and saltpeter. It also sailed to Bengal and Masulipatam. The ship continued in service until February 1659, when it left Madras on a homeward voyage to England and was lost at sea.

⁵ President Aaron Baker had been an agent under the president at Bantam and was made the first governor of the presidency at Fort St. George, 1653–1654. He served several terms at Bantam, being president there in 1640–1643, 1645–1649, 1650–1652, and at Madras in 1652–1655. Baker and his wife were on a voyage to Fort St. George when she died at sea about ten days after they left Bantam. Her tombstone is still in the cemetery of St. Mary's Church in Fort St. George. Mrs. Baker was a daughter of Ralph Cartwright, president at Bantam, 1643–1645. Baker returned to England in 1655, remarried, and settled in Devonshire; he died October 28, 1683. The ship *Roebuck* was about 250 tons. She had arrived at Fort St. George on September 2, 1652. Fear of the Dutch caused the *Roebuck* and the *Lanneret* to sail together to Persia; in a fight with three Dutch ships there, the *Roebuck* lost her foremast, caught fire, and was captured, and the *Lanneret* surrendered. The *Roebuck* was rebuilt by the Dutch and renamed the *Utrecht*.

VII

The following was evidently a brief covering letter for a report on the ship's progress since leaving Surat on its voyage to East Africa. That may have been the account reproduced in section VI, although the information given in it is closely parallel to that given here, leading us to wonder at the repetition. The cosigner of the letter, Richard Aston, was to succeed Buckeridge in case of his death.

Worshipfull & [incomplete salutation]

By the inclosed, being [a] Copie of my Letter left here for the Comaunder will acquaint yow with what hath hapned since our leaveing Surratt to which wee intreat yow bee refered. Soe haveing advised yow that we are now bound for Sena, Sofalla & Cape Corintas where we hope by Gods assistance to have dispatched our businesse soe timely as to bee here againe in June & take A Pilate here to cary us to Pate. For by experience wee finde that Coast Soe dangerouse [1] that it is not to bee dealt with with out one. With ye Due tender of our humble Service to your worthy acceptances we obsequeously subscribe

Johana Jan 22th   your observant Servants
                     NB: RA
                             Richard Aston
                     [signature written in later in
                                       another hand]

---

[1] This is probably another reference to the strong current flowing through the Mozambique Channel and also to the many shoals, rocks, and islands on the wide continental shelf at this area along the coast.

VIII

Mr. Austin, being ill, is perhaps asking in this memorandum that Richard Aston make note of the goods consigned to him. It was probably done so that in case of his death, the clearing of his estate could proceed more easily. The second part of the list, dated April 11 though entered in the letter book after the page dated April 25, shows the gifts given to the governor of Mozambique and to the king's factor, during Buckeridge's second voyage.

Remembrance ffrom Mr Austin when hee lay Sick: Aprill ye 25th 1653 consigind to him 3 Baletts [small bales]

   1 Pallumposts [1] 10 corge of Girdars   RA
   1 Chinsts: 2: 15 pieces fugarees [figured cloth]
   1 Dutty: 1:00 Corge moody Boy   RA
     Byrams: 0:09 wet in chest Girdars
   1 parcell Malgees in Chest [containing?]
   2 pieces dereabands [2]
   3 Deal Salloos 3 Pallumposts
Left at Bussora [3] with Jno. Orme
   1 Bahar broune Salloos: 10 corge at 20 rups [4]
   1 Bahar Fertt Ck Browne 9 corge 28½ —
Sent to Persia by Mr. Griffin [5]
   95 corge Browne Adgrees
   20 corge Deal Salloos

---

[1] Perhaps palempore, a kind of chintz cloth.
[2] Deribands (dereabends) was a white cotton cloth from the East Indies, in length about 9 ells, in breadth ⅞ of an ell, or roughly 11 yards by 1 yard.
[3] Basra (Bussora) is a port at the far end of the Persian Gulf. It has an unhealthful climate, and the summer heat is very intense. It served as an early trading port of the East India Company in Persia.
[4] Rupee (Rups), the monetary unit of India, was represented by a silver coin valued at about 2s 6d.
[5] Roger Griffin was at various times in charge of the ship *Supply*, the ship *Hinde*, and the ship *Falcon*. During the Dutch and English fighting the *Falcon* was surrendered to the Dutch. Wounded, Griffin returned to Surat on the ship *Dove*.

Note that I have cleered accounts with Bynge. My goods with Jno. Orme etc. will Clere with Metrodas Persotum & upwards deduct from Malgees Bill: my Bahar Byrams returned. Demaund an Accountt of Jno. Goodyar [6] of ye piece Cloth & desire him to make my estate & my Brothers home to him.

11th

Aprill ye 11th Anno 1653 sent Don ffransisco de Lyma [7] Governer of Mosambiq A Present Vizt

3 Jars Olives	5
2 Bottles Oyle Olive	5
1 Case Spiritts	8
4 Amber hafted knives	4
6 Plain knives	2
2 Raysor Pen knives	1
1 Chesheer Cheese	3½
1 Bag Pista Nutts [pistachio nuts]: 23:lb	3½
A stick [cane] & gloves	8
	40

12th

Sent ye kings Factor	
1 Jar Olives	2½
1 Bottle Oyle	2½
2 Amber knives	2
4 Plain knives	1 0/0
2 Raysor Pen knives	1
2 Boxes Marmalath [marmalade]	2
	11

[6] "Among those who have served many years in these parts is John Goodyear. He came forth a youth, but has long been employed as an assistant at Macao, Basra, and in Persia, and three years ago a salary was assigned to him amongst others" (O.C. Dup 2147). He continued in service at Surat and in Bombay, and finally returned to England in 1668 or 1669.

[7] Francisco de Lima was a Portuguese captain appointed to the governorship of Mozambique. He persuaded the authorities to continue reconstruction of the fort.

IX

The following undated section does not seem to pertain to the pages which precede or follow it.

Haveing conference with some Mores that were Mariners, belonginge to the Portugalls vesell that came in with us from Ingumbane, they complained of ye Portugalls forceing them to serve them & Pilot them to ye ports on these coasts, alouinge amongst 20 of them but three Bahars of goods, Paups, ffrtt [freight], & toll free for there voyages Pay, which may bee 6, 8 or 9 Months makeinge, which may import in Indea 750 Ms. and at Mosambiq about 1200 Ms. Yet had they free liberty to dispose thereof they should be reasonable gainers, for in the Ship they came in was brought 84 Bahars of Ivory which was bought for 8: or 10: Bahars Paups & 3 or 4 Bahars fine Brawles & 20 Bales Beads [containing?] about 120 Mds. Surratt, all which could not cost in Indea 80000 Ms. & ye Ivory is there worth above 80000: Ms., upwards of: 10 for one. Something nere which computacion I have experemented it to bee trew, for in ye river of Save [1] very nere that place my servant bought for A piece byrams as much Ivory as was worth 8 times its value in Suratt.

A Friend of mine tould me that A little after I went last from Mosambiq hee made A voyage for ye late governer Alvora de Sousa [2] Into ye Bay of Larenzo Marques [3] in 25 ½ degrees So. & brought thence

  90 Bahars Ivory importing by estimacion Starling [sterling] 8460
         300 ounces Amber grece — 600
                  lb: 9060

---

[1] This river rises in Southern Rhodesia, flowing east-southeast into the Mozambique Channel.
[2] Álvaro de Sousa de Távora was appointed captain and governor in 1646.
[3] Referred to by Buckeridge as the Bay of Lorenzo Marques, now Delagoa Bay. Founded by the Portuguese in 1544, the seaport of Lourenço Marques has an excellent harbor.

X

A list of material from several packages of Company goods. These are probably items which were sold at each of the ports mentioned.

Taken out of Severall Bales of ye Companys
3 corge Paups on ye Coast of Sofalla
1 corge Byrams on Ditto
2 corge Paups at Mosambiq
3½ corge Baftas at Johanna
1 corge Braw: 13 besa [1] at Johanna
4 pieces besotas [2] at Ditto
1 corge 13 besas & besotas at Queloa
10 pieces Baftas ⎫
10 pieces Byrams ⎬ att Ditto
10 pieces Rosse [3] ⎪
20 pieces Paups ⎭
2 pieces Besotas at Mosambiq sould
1 Corge Chaw [4] cource I think Benga at Johanna
   at Mowanda: [5]
17 corge Paups:
2 = Baftas
2: Byrams
1 corge Braw: Ross
   at Zinzebar
3 corge Cource Chaw Bengala
1 corge Sorts 13 beesa at Pemba

---

[1] Bezan (Besa, beesa) was a cotton cloth from Bengal. Some pieces were white, others were striped with several colors.
[2] Besutos (besotas) was a kind of hairy cotton cloth.
[3] Chabnam, or rosee, was a kind of muslin or very fine and clear cotton cloth, from the East Indies, especially Bengal. It was 16 ells long and ⅔ or ¾ of an ell wide (20 yards long by about 1 yard wide).
[4] Chautar (chaw) was a large piece of cloth, sheet or shawl, white or in colors.
[5] Perhaps Mowana, a branch of the mouth of the Rufiji River which enters the Mozambique Channel near the island of Mafia.

XI

The following continues Buckeridge's letter dated January 22, 1653 (item VII), through May 23, 1653. Again the recipient is not named, but it most surely was meant for the president of the Company at Surat. President Blackman, in a letter to the Company in England, writes that "wee had letters from Mr. Buckeridge that is Cheife Merchant upon her [the *Assada Merchant*] dated the fine of August last, who then Certified us of there well being in Patta . . ." (O.C. 2352).

Worshipfull & Worthy ffriends

My last left at Johanna, bearing Date ye 22th Jan, will advise yow of all occurences till that time. Wherefore I shall now omitt repetition therof because ye conveyance is Dubeous & wilbe tedious. Yet it cannot bee unnecesary to adventure this breife letter to advise yow that after leaveing Johanna wee intended to Spend some time on ye Coast of Sofalla befor wee went for Augustine Bay. And being upon that Coast in about 17 degrees latitude wee were forced to ride out A very ffirce & violent storme wherin Gods mercys were very great to us in preserving us. & when it broke up after 48: hours rageing we found our Ruder broke short of [f] at ye uper most Pintle.[1] & when they had: an observacion they found themselves 10 Leagus to ye So. of ye latitude they came to Anchor in. Haveing strengthened our Rader ye best we could we hastned for ye river of Sena in 18 deg: So. hopeing there to repair it better. And comeing there: ye Portugalls were amazed at our unexpected arivall thither but were Seemingly Curteous & ready to help us but pretended that they had noe body that could Pilot us over ye Bar. & ye Master would not ventur over with out one. But for mater of trade they dare not deale with us with out leave from ye Governer of Mosambiq. Soe wee hasted thence for Ingumbane, about: 21: deg So. in hopes there to Supply our wants. But pasing by that for fear of foule weather wee intended to continew Coasting to 24½ deg be-

---

[1] The pintle is a pin forming part of the hinge of a rudder, usually placed upright in the sternpost, to hold the brace of the rudder.

fore wee put over for Augustine Bay, but were taken with a storme beefore we could raise that latitude, that forct us to leward of ye shoules of ye Jews.[2] & being past hopes of gaining ye Bay & in A bad Condicon to beat it up in expectacion of other winds we bore up for Mosambiq ye 22th March & Arived here ye 7th Aprill. At my comeing on Shore I was kindly enterteined by ye Governer who promised his assistance to Suply our wants & that wee should have ffree liberty to depart when we thought ffit & if we sould any goods wee should pay but 5 per Cent Customs. But this Agreement should only bee for this time. Hereafter wee must not come without ye Vice Roys leave. Upon which incoragement I tooke A house & landed some goods to trey ye marketts. But noene made profers to buy saying they stayd till ye Governer had opened ye price, who fell Sick imediatly upon our coming & could not bee spoken withall till ye 13th present when hee was willing to deal with me conditionaly that I would stay for payment till ye returne of his Sena Ship as it is his accustomary time of payment to all that hee deals with or else to pay me by bills of exchange in Goa, or to make my payment heere next year in what Speties I would at A considerable rate. For ye Sena Ship it is A hazard whither she gains her voyage or not. & if shee dos shee is not expected to returne till August which wilbe to late for Us to goe into ye read Sea accordinge to your order. Soe that I cannot accept of any of his profers without an expresse breach of your comition. Wherefore I am forct to deney him though hee proffers on these Conditions to deal with me for ye whole Cargo. Wherefore I have taken his leave to bee Goeing & intend by Gods assistance to sett saile to morow morning for Johanna. Haveing imbarqd all things from ye Shore with out sale of any thing saveing part of ye Asada trade which wilbe Suffitient to defray our Charges. I am ye readilier prompted to A quick departure by ye arivall of A Ship from Goa ye 15: Current of ye Governers who sett saile thence ye 10th March. Ye governer hath this year 3: Ships arived from Goa for his oune Accountt. From whence here is 2: Ships for Accountt of divers marchants & one belonging to Bamans. Here is more one Ship from Dew, in all 7, ye least wherof is upwards of 200 Tunns. Soe that here is A Glut of All Comodities save provisions which bear an exces-

---

[2] The Bassas da India, Baxos da India, or Shoals of India, located between the mainland and the island of Madagascar, is a circular coral reef about six miles in diameter enclosing a shallow lagoon. Currents in its vicinity are strong and many ships were lost there. Portuguese discoverers named it the Baxios de Judia; the name was afterwards corrupted by the English into Bassas da India.

sive rate. And ye Choule Ship intended hither is Cast away som 60 Leagus to ye No. of this place.

    1653
    May: 19th

P S: My Letter being Sealed & all things imbarqued, ye Governer sent for me & tould me I must needs Gratifie him in staying two or 3: days longer. Which I was very unwilling to assent to but knowing noe remedy in regaurd of his Sena Ships late departure I consented to his desires or rather comaundes & could not get my dispatch till this day. Soe haveing advised yow of the Death of my asistant Richard Aston & Wm. Browne Boatswain, both in this place, ye ffirst ye 23th Ulto ye other ye 19th present. & one Jno. Hunter who was transhipt from ye Suply [3] is runn Away. I once againe take leave to Subscribe

May: 23th 1653   your Idem Servant

---

[3] The ship *Supply*, about 250 tons, was the first Indian-built ship that sailed to England. She had been engaged in bringing settlers to Assada and in taking refugees from that plantation to Surat. She had sailed to Basra, Gombroon, and Bantam.

XII

This rather long letter from Johanna is a complete résumé of the entire trip from departure to June 24, 1653. Information regarding navigation and weather problems is included, as well as their reception at the various ports and their attempts at trade. The last page of the letter contains a brief account of the Assada plantation failure.

Worshipfull & Worthy ffriends

After our Departure with Shipp ffalcon [1] off of Dew, we Shaped our cource for ye Coast of Melin[de] intendinge by Gods asistance for Pate (conceiveing in probabilitie that ye monsoon would alow us to visitt that Porte before we went for ye Coast of Soffalla:). And saleing with A ffaire wind wee made ye Coast in about 4: deg: No. But ye winds were soe ffresh & ye Currentts soe strong that wee were caried with almost incredible Seleritie [celerity] into: 2: degrees South, though wee made sale only by day and lay A trey all: Night, not seeinge either of ye towns wee saw ye former voyage nor yett discovering any port or or [sic] haven which might probablie bee Pate. Soe wee left that Shore, ye Master being fearfull of embaying [running aground] if hee went any further, & Steered a way for Johana. But were deceaved in ye Curent which they expected to bee ye same in ye offin [offing as] it was by ye Shore. And ye ffirst land we saw after wee left ye Coast of Melinde was ye Island of Cosmoledo [2] of[f] of ye No. end of St. Lawrence where wee could ffinde noe Anchoring but stood away for [steered toward] Johanna. But mising it wee came to an

---

[1] This ship, with a capacity of about 560 tons, sailed between Surat and Gombroon and Basra under master Roger Griffin. She was described as being unstable and needing 2½ to 3 feet of ballast in her hold, thus reducing her cargo capacity. In this particular voyage she was bound for Basra and sailed September 19, 1651, for Surat, arriving there November 1, 1651. In 1653 she was used in the Dutch-English fighting in the Persian Gulf, carrying 26 guns. During a hard battle the ship suffered much damage, the master was wounded, and she was surrendered to the Dutch. All books and letters aboard were lost.
[2] A group of small, low islands in the Indian Ocean north of Madagascar.

Anchor at Comero ³ where we had fare quarter & usage in our trade for provisions. But our Anchor came home from ye place it was laid in [dislodged from its bed] & wee drove into Deepe water & foule grounde in ye night with out perceiveing it. Wee endeavoured with ye helpe of ye Natives to weigh it but could not. Soe ye Master intended to make A windlese to sucour ye Capston ⁴ before hee atemptd again to weigh it. Haveing procured A peece of timber on Shore for that purpose there being noe conveinent roome for it in ye Skiff, [the skiff] being laden with wood, I caused it to bee put into ye long boat, which was laden with water & went of[f] in ye Skiff hopeing to gett abord ye Sooner. But god had otherwise determined & our too much securitie & confidence brought our safety in great hasard, for an unexpected Current drove us A starne & wee could not row against it. But they were more provident in ye Longboat & got safe abord which they unladed with all possible expedition. Yet it was Night ere Shee was clered. When being more sencible of ye Danger wee were in then wee ourselves, who were rowing into ye Shore & in greate hasard to runne upon A desperate Shoule, they cut ye Cable in ye haff & drove shooteing gunns and hallowing till they heard us make answer, being all most extreamly perplexed with ye Sence of ye danger I was in: (God make me thankfull, for my deliverance from it). And being safe on borde we made sale for Johanna & ye next eiveninge came to Anchor in this roade, being ye 21th Jan. And haveinge left your Letters here for ye Europ Ships, wee sett saile for sena, intending thence for Ingomabane & Cape Corintas before we went for Augustine Bay. Haveinge Calme weather it was ye 4th Ffebrr before we Came to ye Islands of Angosa,⁵ som 16½ degrees, where we spent some days ffruitlesse & whence we made A slow progresse for Sena. & being clere of the Islands in upwards: of 17: degrees ffebr ye 17th, the wind blew hard & being unwilling to leave the shore wee came to An Anchor in about 12 ffathams water some 3: leagus from shore, hopeinge it would soone bee over. But it increased to A very ffirce & violent storme mixed with raine that we could not see the shore all the time it Continewed being: 48 howers. The Seas runne very high & ffomed exceedingly in soe muchas ye

---

³ It is the northwesternmost and largest of a group of four islands called the Comoros, another of which is Johanna. The four islands have a total area of 790 square miles.

⁴ The windlass was a strong column of timber for bringing in the anchor cable. It coils the cable vertically, the capstan coils it horizontally.

⁵ Ilha Angoche lies south of Mozambique, just off its coast.

water which at our comeinge to Anchor was clere became as mudie as it is usualie in swaly hole. And when the storme abated & ye Aire cleered we discovered an adition to our affliction, for our Ruder was broke short of[f] at ye uper Pintle, which we mended ye best we could hopeing to repair it better at Sena. Haveinge taken An observacion thay found them selves droven 10 leagus to ye Southward of ye place we came to Anchor in & soe much we drove in ye storme, wherein Gods mercys were very great in preserving us and wee are exceedinglie bound to acknowledge them with harty thankfullnesse. Discovering A river we weighed & stood neerer into ye shore & sent our boat to inquier what place it was & how far Sena was thence. And they tould us that River was called Lungosa [Lualua River?] & ye river of sena[6] was 2 days Journy more Southward. Saileing forward we discovered more rivers and A low wodie Countrie without any remarkable land. & our depths of water was most comonly soe many ffathams as wee were miles from ye Shore. The: 24th ffebr it pleased god to bring us safe to Anchor before the Rivers mouth of Sena, about in: 18: deg, where sending our boat on Shore to inquire certanlie whither it were the place or not. Our People mistakeinge their message went up to Chelemana ye Port towne some: 12: Miles up ye river where the Portugalls & Musteefas, about 20: persons with 2 or 300 Caferees, being amazed at our unexpected comeinge were all in armes. But perceiving our People came not in an hostile manner they received them peaceablie & treated with them, who tould them wee were bound for Augustine bay with advices for our Europe Shipps haveing warrs with ye Dutch. & haveinge mett with A Great Storme on this coast & broke our Ruder [we] desired A Pilote to bring us into ye River that wee might mend it. There Answer was that there was noe Pilots below, they were all at Sena, & that they were unfurnished with People or Materialls to acomodate us, but advised us to goe to Mosambiq where we might bee Supplied. The next day I went on Shore to trey if I could prevaile with them. They entertained me curteousle & profered all the helpe they could if we would come in but contineued to deney that they had anybody to Pilot us in. And for matter of tradeing with us they dar not medle in it with out leave from ye Governer of Mosambiq. Goeing on board I advised with ye Master what was best to bee donne, who was willinge to goe in but would once more send in ye boat to discover a beter channell & bring off her ladeinge of water

---

[6] The present Zambezi River, its mouth at approximately 18° South.

which shee returned with, but discovered noe channell & ye best depth wee discovered on ye barr in 3 times goeing in & comeing out was: 2¼ ffadam, though doubtlesse there is A better Channell, for to my knowledge A Shipp hath gonne in here whose draught of water was more than 2¼ ffa. But our boat rows soe heavily & badly that wee could make noe beter discovery of it than wee did without wastinge more time & runninge further hasards of rideinge there which wee were loath to doe upon soe slight incoragment. Sena it Selfe the towne of tradee is som 40 or 50 [crossed out: 30 or 40] Leagus further up the River, which they ordenarylie make 10 or 15 days Journey of with their laden flat botomd boats against ye streame. It is by report A faire Citie & Rich. But theire Cheife strength consists in their Slaves, wherof they have very Many & I beleive are there better ffurnished with white men than anyplace in these parts, for it is A place of very great trade rather exceeding than comeinge Shorte of ye relacion I gave yow last voyage, And might easilie bee drawne hence for ye Coast is full of rivers and I beleive as good as this though hapilie it hath been better. Butt now the Portugalls doe generally complain of ye badnesse of ye Barr whither in policie or realitie I cannot tell or out of ye Sence of the great losse they lately had in ye late Governers vesell which was there cast away. But if another Nation were setled in any of the adjacent Rivers, which hapilie maybe branches of ye same that this is, doubtlesse the Natives would easilie bee intreated to buy where they could have ye best penyworths.

Pri: Mar:

ffebr: ye ulto: wee weighed Anchor from ye rivers mouth of Sena intendinge to passe by Sofalla & to endeavour for Ingumbane. Comeinge againe into ye Shore wee made the land in 20½ degr. Wee discovered A river & sent ashore our boate & ye Natives informed us that that river was called Save, A days Journy to ye So. of Soffalla: & 2: days Journey to ye No. of Ingumbane. Soe that I judge Soffalla to ley in a litle upwards of 20: & Ingumbanne of 21 deg S. Weighing thence wee [sailed] A little ffurther & discovered an other River whither wee sent our boate. And they tould us ye name of it was Seefa [7] & that if wee would goe up ye river wee should have plenty of Eliphants teeth & that A Portugall Boat was gonne up some: 2: or 3 days before that

---

[7] Perhaps the river flowing northward into a small bay just below the Save River.

came from Sofalla to trade with that kinge. & Ingumbane was soe nere that they profered to goe in A Prow Along with our boat & shew it them poynting & telling them it was in A Bay beyond that poynt which they Shewed them. Thence wee weighed ye winds blouing fresh. We sailed by it to my great greife though I could not helpe it for it Pleased God thus to ffrustrate my endeavours & disanimate our People by our severall disasters that they could not bee induced to adventure soe far as in my apprehention they might safely have donne. But being weake & unexperienced in these affairs I did as my only remedie Patiently Submitt to Gods divine Pleasure & theire Judgments.

After this I importuned the Master & c[rew] to continew coasting to Cape Corintas & though we discovered noe Porte before we dubled it yett still to continew & endeavour for ye bay of Lorenzo Marques betwene 25: & 26: deg. But [I] found A Generall Unwillingnesse to venture further than 24½ deg. & before we had raised that lattitude wee were taken with A storm & steering for Augustine Bay drove soe to leward that we could not weather ye Shouls of the Jews, but were forced to bear up. & Conceiveing it fruitles to endeavour further for Augustine Bay, we Joyntly thought it best to goe for Mosambiq & thither Shaped our cource March ye 22th. But [we] were soe aposed by A Curentt in about 17 deg latitude that we arived not thithere till ye 7th Aprill. At our comeinge on Shore there ye Governer, being preadvised of our being at Sena, seemed som what displeased therewith, but soone waved that discource haveinge noe just objections against it & profered us all things that hee could procure to Supplie our wantes (being increased by A defect in our bowsprit soe great that it was unfitting to goe to sea with without A fish on it[8]). & on my request hee publiqlie promised me that I should have libertie to goe thence when I thought fitt & in mater of Customs to favour me what hee could. Wher upon we came under comaund & visiting him upon our comeing in I treated with him about ye Customs. & hee willinglie asented to take 5 per Cent: & clere me from all Duties whatsoever. Wherwith A [i.e., I] acquainted ye kings ffactor or Customer who seemd contented with what ye Governer had donne, where upon I hired a house, [crossed out: for undeciphered amount per month] &

---

[8] The bowsprit, the mast that projects over the stem, was in need of repair, so they put a fish on it. A fish was a long piece of hard wood, convex on one side and concave on the other. Two of them were bound opposite each other to strengthen the mast. To do this they were well secured by bolts and hoops, or stout rope called woolding.

landed some goods in hopes of Marketts which were not then opened. Nither could (or would) any man tell me wherabouts the price might bee. Some marchants of Qualitie veiued the goods & liked them & comended them but did not (or darst not) make A price of them, it being A custom among them not to buy till ye Governer hath made ye price, who falling sick upon our comeing in was not to bee spoken with, being taken with A very violent feavor in ye time of his sicknesse. One of our men being Drunke in the night was disturbant in ye Streets knocking at mens dores & rambling hee knew not whither. It being very tempesteous, thundering & lighteninge, hee went into A new worke [9] they have almost finished to strengthen ye Castle where ye Dutch formerlie made A Batery & falling thence broke his leg. & though hee knows not how hee went thether or fell thence his [he] was soe sencible after his fall as to craule to A watch house & Sheltred him selfe there till morninge without knowledge of the sentinells. But early in the Morninge they [were] acquainted of one of our peoples beinge there & his disaster & desired me to take care of him, which I did with all Posible Speede, but could not get our boat & Chirirgion [surgeon] on Shore Soone enough, for ye Castle Gates being open & ye governer haveinge notice of it caused him to bee brought into the Castle. & sent for me & demaunded of me what Justice we used in our Countrie to A man that Scaled Castle walls in ye night. I could not deney but if he were an enemy that did it, hee deserved Death but wee were friends & this was an Act of Drunkennese & not malice & deserved not soe severe A punishment. Wherefore I intreated him to release him since God had all ready punished him. Hee tould me hee beleived what I alledged but deneyed my request. Nither would hee let ye Chirirgion come to him till hee had further examinned him because hee must give an accountt thereof to ye vizeroy.

Soone after this John hunter, one of our men that was transhipt from ye Suplie, tooke ocasion to run away & reported to ye Governer, as I am informed, that wee had 10: Ships at Augustine bay intended hither to take ye Castle & wee were come for Spies. Which report was seconded by some Souldiers which tould him that ye pased eiveninge I sent things out of ye house to Sr Jacinta Cocteens A reputed frind of mine, & of all English that come thither, & our boat was seene that

---

[9] Probably the four-bastioned fortress of S. Sebastiao, begun in 1558, one of the strongest and most important Portuguese forts. It fell into disrepair and was rebuilt in the seventeenth century.

night rovinge to & again to sound ye harbour, & that ye Shipp now rod A Peeke [directly over the anchor] & was ready to sett saile. The Governer haveing sent for me by 2 souldiers like A Delinquent demaunded of me the reason why I did such things as hee was informed of me. All which I uterly deneyd being altogither ffalce. Hee gave noe credit to my answer at present but was betwixt Anger & weaknesse very passionate & bid me goe to my house & live at Quiet till hee had further examined ye mater. I tould him hee should not neede to bid me doe that for I nither had donne or would doe otherwise, but I was sorry to see hee had such ill People about him to trouble him with such falce & Impertinent reports in his Sicknesse. & being Againe deneyd our lame man haveing demaunded him I tooke leave of him for that time.

By reason of ye Governers Sicknesse I could not treat with him about sale of our goods till ye 13: May when hee was willinge to deal with mee conditionaly, that I would stay for payment till ye returne of his Sena Ship, as it is his accustomary time of payment to all that hee deals with, or elce to pay me by bills of exchange in Goa or to make my payment heere next year in what Speties I would at A considerable rate. For ye Sena Ship it is A hasard whither She gains her Voyage or not & if shee dos shee is not expected to retourne till August which wilbe to late for us to goe into ye read Sea accordinge to your order. Soe that I cannot accept of any of his profers without an expresse breach of your comition. Wherfore I am forct to deney him though hee proffers on these Conditions to deal with mee for ye whole Cargo. But his returnes from Sena would not be Suffitient to discharge his other ingagements. Wherefore I refused his profers & desired his lisence to depart. To which he semed willing, yett in respect of his Sena Shipps late departure hence hee dare not trust us, but found devices to deteine us till ye 23th May. There are arived seaven vesells hither this yeare 6 from Goa: vizt 3 for the Governers owne Accountt, 2 for other marchants & one for Accountt of Bannians & one from Dew, in which are come soe much goods that noe man profered to buy or aske the price of ours. Nither have I sould any thinge, save my part of the Assada trade, suffitient to defray our expences. I was very desireous to gett thence soe soone as I could in regaurd of the Contageousnesse of the place, the major part of the People being Sick & Mr. Richard Aston & our Boatswain dead, ye Gunners mate runn Away & At Mosambiq & our Boatswains mate died since we came to Johanna. But I privatlie brought away 5 Goa lascars from Mosambiq which are A great helpe to us. They came all lately from Ingumbanne

& give A very good report of the place affirming it to aford annyally at least 50 or 60 Bahars of Ivory & 2 or 300 ounces ambergreece importing about 4000 lb at very easy rates. It being the Governer of Mosambiqs order that noe man shall give more than 10 pieces Paups for A tooth that weighs a ffrasula [10] [containing?] about 29 lb: weight which is nere 10 times the price of the Cloth in Indea, to which place ye Portugalls yearly voyage but have noe settled residence.

At Mosambiq I was informed, by my acquaintance that were factors for ye late Governer to Cape Corintas, that they brought thence 90 Bahars Ivory & 2 or 300 ounces of Ambergreece their last voyage. & soe much that Port usualy afords every: 2: years. Ye place of trade being on an Island [11] in the Bay of Lorenso Marques in upwards of 25 degrees So. on which place ye Portugalls have noe residence, but voyage thither once in two years from Mosambiq. Whither ye Governer is prepareing this year to send. If it Pleased God that wee had arived at either Mirca,[12] Patte, Ingumbane, or ye Bay of Lorenso Marques wee had in probalilitie [sic] made A very profitable vouge. But God hath otherwise determined. Wherfore I crave your patience & intreat yow to rest assured that my endeavors nither have been nor shalbe wanting, when god shall blesse me with an opportunitie. It hath pleased god yett to add to our former unhappinesse, for our sheat Anchor [13] is foule of A rock & I fear wee shall loose him. But I have here provided 3 stonn kellaks [14] & intend by Gods help to make A new Bass Cable when We come to Pate, whether by Gods help wee are now bound haveing taken Pilots here & intend to visit Pemba in the way, haveing staid till now to fitt ourselvs & in expectacion of ye Coast Ships arivall hither from England. Wherof wee are now out of hopes: haveing lost 4 of our men, one being lame & uselesse for this voyage being tortered by ye Portugalls in ye time of his inprisonment, being hanged up by ye lame leg & bound about the head to confesse the fellow knows not what. Nither could hee give them any Answer not knowing theire language And many others of our men sick & weak I

---

[10] Frasilah, a weight used in the East, varying from 12 to 35 pounds. A bahar equals 20 frasilah.
[11] Inhaqua Island, a center of trade.
[12] Merca (Morca), a coastal Arab town between Brava and Magadoxa.
[13] A large anchor, formerly always the largest of a ship's anchors, used only in an emergency.
[14] A kellagh was a wooden anchor with a stone in it, but in later times the term was applied to any grapnel or small anchor.

feare that we shall not venture into ye read Sea to seeke ye Decan veselle,[15] if wee finde trade where we are now bound which these People tell us wee need not doubt of. Yet I hope with Gods helpe to bee with yow some time in October.

 Haveinge had Conference with some marchants in this place that I used to trade to Assada & inquireing of them for what reason ye king of that place (who is now dead) did massacar our People, who informed me that ye cheife reason was to bee revenged of ye injurie donne him by Tho: Page etc. in Shipp James,[16] haveing Cosoned him with falce Ryalls which Mr. Mosse made at Augustine Bay in ye time of Esquire Corteens Planters resideing there, which Colonell Hunt [17] promised to make good to him but failed in his performance therof, soe that according to heathen justice hee had a ffair pretence for his villany. Thus I desire to put A period to this tragicall description & hope god will blesse us with better successe in the ffuture. & haveing presented humble Service to your favourable acceptances I obseqously Subscribe

Joh: June ye 24th 1653   Your observant Servant

---

[15] Decan is the southern peninsula of India, especially the tableland between eastern and western Ghats. In the sixteenth century the Portuguese applied the term to the Mohammedan kingdom of Bijapur. The Decan merchants probably made an annual voyage from India to Africa.

[16] This ship was in the employ of the Courten Company, rivals of the East India Company. Her capacity was about 700 tons. Thomas Page sailed on the *James* to Mocha in June of 1646, the same year that she was sold at Goa.

[17] Colonel Robert Hunt was the governor of the group attempting to establish a plantation on Assada in 1649. He died there sometime the next year.

XIII

Written at Johanna on the same day as the preceding, the following short letter is meant for the crew of a ship coming from England. This can be inferred because Buckeridge notes "the President & Councell inordered us to leave the inclosed letter from them to yow either at Augustine Bay: or here."

Worthy ffriends

Pinnace Asada marchant being bound on A discovery of ye Coasts of Melinde & Sofalla, the President & Councell inordered us to leave the inclosed letter from them to yow either at Augustine Bay: or here. We formerly intended to have left it at ye former place (& itts transcript here). But haveinge Coasted the Coast of Sofalla from 16 to 24 degrees we intended to Stand over for Augustine Bay, but could not for we were forct in A Storme to bear up for Mosambiq whence we are returned hither again & have staid many day here expecting yow. But being out of hopes of your arrival till August wee are intended hence by Gods helpe for Pate, where wee hope to heare from yow before we goe thence, here being A vesell belonging to that place. Wherefore lett me intreat yow to Advise me whither we have warr or peace with ye Dutch or Portugalls, & deliver your Letter unto this bearer who intends to voyage thither. It will much importe me to heare from yow, that I may ye beter regulate my selfe in my comeinge on ye Coast of Indea, for I heare both at Mosambiq & this place that after we left Suratt, being ye 13 December, the Dutch & we have had A Broyle & fought in Swally hole. But ye Governer of Suratt hath taken up ye mater & disgraced ye Dutch, fforbiding them on paine of Banishment to molest ye kings Porte, & leavs them to their liberty on the Seas. I doe not much credit ye report, houever thought fitt to advise yow of it, that yow may prepare to prevent ye worst. Pray afford transport to ye inclosed unto ye President & Councell as directed. Soe with my prayers for our happie incounter in Swally hole, I comitt yow [to] ye protection of ye Almighty & humblie rest

Johanna June 24th　　　　　　　　　your very loving ffriend
1653　　　　　　　　　　　　　　　　　　　　　N.B.

XIV

In this undated account of goods, the "Natta" is unidentified. The material following "Dear maddam" is not in Buckeridge's hand. A brief list of merchants at Pate and Muscat follows it.

Dr [debitor]	Natta	Cr [creditor]	
To: 1 piece Sussee[1]	5:½	By mony borowed	5: —
To: 7 pieces Pallumposts	3:½	By 10½ myn: Tort: Shell:	18:½
To: 1½ corge Steele	2½	By 4 Slaves	30: — [40]
	11½		63½[2]
To cash: paid him	42 [52]	By mony borowed	
	63½		

pd 32   Dear maddam

I have taken the boldnes to troubel you wit

At Pate ye Cheife marchants are Longe Corge Sas sonn: Congees, & Nog gees sonns hassan Matacca. Brokers: Samma scinde & Lona at Mircat. Ye Governers Amudabas & Noor Abas Merchants: Ahmud hodge Ameen & Shereef A deen: Otman ye 4 Beemalls or Buddoos: Mahmud Abrahim Hantro.

---

[1] Soosy, a mixed striped fabric of silk and cotton in India.
[2] Both of these totals should be 53½; 52 was changed to 42 and 40 to 30 without the totals being changed.

XV

This long letter of November 30 continues the narration of the second voyage, begun in a letter of June 24, 1653, transcribed here as item XIII. The major events occurring after the departure from Johanna to the ship's arrival at Bassein are given including an account of a very bad storm encountered on the voyage.

Worshipfull & Worthy ffriends

Haveing left at Johanna your Letters for ye outerbound ships & A relacion directed to yow adviseing all occurances that had happened in our voyage to that time, whose transcript goes here inclosed to which I intreat yow bee refered; we intended to Shape A direct cource for ye Island Pemba. But findeing ye Currents not soe strong as we expected them we stood right over & made ye Main & went into Quiloa, A very Spatious harbour. & ye Next day after our comeing in I went to ye towne in quest of trade. But ye king of Pemba his fleete had lately been there & fired ye towne which is on an Island soe that ye Major part of ye inhabitants were dispersed on ye Main & only 10 or: 15 Portugalls & A fewe People that came with them in A vesell from ye So. ye day before us, & A remnent of ye Natives that had most of them relacion to ye Portugalls remained in ye ruins some of whome made profers to trade with us but were by ye Portugalls soe over eyed & over awed them that they darst not. Being that & ye next day prevented by ye Portugalls from speaking with ye king, which was on ye Main, I sought ye third day by another means to come to Speech of him & sent our Pilot & an Arab that I brought from Johanna with A present to him & desired to have admittance in to his presence & to trade with him. But hee would not bee spoken with nor receive ye Present nor yett trade with us, saing it was A bad time useing some other expressions denoteing him willing to trade with us but darst not by reason ye Portugalls were there, who either diswaded or hindred him from its being as I suppose entered into a more strict League than formerly with them to be revenged of ye king of Pemba for ye injury late donne him. But his sonne semed displeased at it & said if we came another time & if his father would not trade with us he would. It is by all reports A place of good trade but ye king is soe intangled in Covenants with ye Portugalls that he cannot well clere himselfe of them. Hee is by covenant yearly to take soe much cloth of ye Governer of Bombasse & to pay him soe many Bahars Ivory at A sett rate. But to what import I am not well informed. Ye Governers of Mombass hath accustomarily his factors resideing there. But ye 2 passed years they dare not stay all ye year by reason of there wars with ye king of Pemba who hath donne them much mischeif. I was alsoe tould by A Portugall there that ye Governer of Bombasse farms ye trade of that place for 15000 Sherateens [1] for ye tearm of his Government, being 3 years, & in like manner he farms other places of trade on ye Coast, but for what soms I know not. It is A usuall custom with ye Portugalls, for ye late Governer of Mosambiq at my former being there tould me hee farmd his 3 years government there for 100000 Crusados, 20000 lb Starling. Perceaving our endeavours frusterate haveing spent 3 days fruitles we made sale thence for Pemba intending to goe without ye Island of Zinzebar fearing ye iner passage [2] to be dangerous, but were by tides & Curentts put on ye Main again. Not knowing it but supposing our selvs sailing alongst ye outer side of Zinzebar we espied an Island which we tooke to be Pemba. But sailing to it found it to be Zinzebar where ye People were very shey & cautious to be spoken with, fearing that we were Portugalls their enemies, but were at last persuaded by our Pilot to speak & deal with us. When perceiving our manner of dealing they were joyfull of our comeing wishing we would come yearly, saying they had rather give us their goods than sell them to ye Portugalls & gave us A Pilot to conduct us to that part of ye Island where ye better part of ye inhabitants were convented [residing]. & sailing thither we passed by ye ruins of ye Towne [3] where ye Queene of ye Island & ye Portugalls formerly inhabited, & was that Part of it that belonged to ye Portugalls ruined by ye king of Pembas Souldiers

---

[1] A xerafine was a silver coin used at Goa and other eastern ports; its value was a little less than ls 6d.

[2] The passage between the mainland and the island of Zanzibar is about twenty miles wide but very shallow, for the most part barely twenty fathoms deep.

[3] The town was destroyed by Francisco de Seixas Cabreira in 1652 when he led an expedition from Mombasa after the Oman's ships had raided Zanzibar and sacked the Portuguese settlement. Cabreira released 400 Christians who had been captured by the enemy; later the Portuguese rebuilt the church and reoccupied the factory there.

assisted by some Arrabbs of Muscatt [4] Anno: 1651, when they slew & Captivated 50 or 60 Portugall men & women & tooke much spoyle about 50 Bahars Ivory & much other goods. & ye other part belonging to ye Queene & Natives was ruined in May last by ye Governer of Mombas ffransisco Shesha [5] who came thither as reported with 23 [changed from 43] saile of vessells in which were 450 Portugalls & 1200 Caferes of ye main wherwith hee hath ruined ye Island & slain many of ye People & taken from them well nigh as rich A Spoyle as ye king of Pemba tooke from them ye former year in revenge wherof hee hath donn this because they would not assist ye Portugalls against ye king of Pembas souldiers & ye Arrabbs & hath carried Captive to Bombasse well nigh A: 1000 of ye Natives. Coming to ye Place where ye remaining Natives resided I found them well Nigh famished being hindred by ye wars from tilling ye ground & readier to buy with what little goods they had left provisions than Clothing if I had had it for them. Ye Queene haveing left ye Island was gone to ye Main to Joyne forces with A Neibouring Prince against Another Prince on ye Main that had assisted ye Portugalls Against them. Being importuned by her Deputie & ye Marchants & willing therto of my selfe I wrote to ye Quene & to ye king of ye Main desireing to treat [changed from "contract"] & trade with them who returned me Curteous answers & sent one to treat with me. For tradeing they could not then medle with their warning being soe short & they soe imbroyled in their wars, but assured me we should have ffree & fair dealing there when ever we came thither. But ye Cheife import of his message was to procure our Assistance in their wars to assalt their enemies Port & fire their vessells, wher with they much anoyd them, which I refused & tould him my comition was only for trade & I darst not atempt any such thing without leave from yow, with which answer hee was satisfied & desired me to come again next year, & I need not fear to finde good tradeing but I must come thither some time before may & reside 2: or 3 months.

---

[4] This city in Arabia, on the Gulf of Oman, is located directly under the Tropic of Cancer. It was the center of Portuguese power in the area, but in spite of virtually impregnable fortifications, it fell to the imam of Oman in 1650.

[5] Francisco de Seixas Cabreira was governor of Mombasa from 1635 to 1639, during which time he led forces that subjugated the Bajun Islands. He commemorated his victory by an inscription, still legible today, above the main gateway of Fort Jesus at Mombasa. Because of the threat posed by the Arabs after their defeat of Muscat in 1650, he was sent back to Mombasa and served a second term as governor from 1651 to 1653.

There it is & hath been by all reports A place of good trade for Ivory, Bees wax, [crossed out: Tortoise Shells: Nuckla] & Sanderoos [6] A Gumm like Amber, all at very Cheap rates & in good quantities. & ye goods yow shall buy them with are truckt of at Duble theire costs & some sorts for more in Indea. And though by reason of their present condicion they had not much now. Yett doubtlesse it may yearly yeild A considerable Quantitie, ye Island leying soe comodiously & nere ye Main from whence they fetch it.

Saileing thence for Pemba wee were again deceived by ye Curentt that setts in betwene ye 2: Islands & put to Leward of our Porte, but got into an other Port on ye Island. & hearing of ye kings great purchases tooken from ye Portugalls & not dealing with them this ii [i.e., 2] years I hoped to finde him full of goods & hungry after trade. Wherefore on his invitacion I journied to him but found it contrary for hee had given ther Arrabbs of Muscatt all ye Ivory hee tooke at Zinzebar in payment for Cloth & other goods bought of them. Yett profered to deall with me if I would send for the goods, which I refused being unwilling to trust him with ye goods & our persons at once, hearing A bad report of him. But tould him I had musters of ye goods with me & if hee would make A price of them & alsoe of ye goods he would pay me in, I would deliver ye goods where ye Shipp road to his people before I received my payment. But he would not accept of my profer nither could I gett leave to goe on bord again till 3 or 4 days after I desired it, by reason of his statelinesse & pretended indisposition to health. & then haveing promised to sell him some things for his owne use I sent them him being unwilling to ffalcifie my promise to him least it might be A hinderance to our future trade with him if we should herafter come thither, for which he made me honest though slow payment. Haveing ye better halfe of our men sick & dead we darst not venture into ye redd sea inquest with ye Decan: Jounks [junks] knowing our unability to deale with one if wee should meet her. & haveing finished what businesse we then could at Pemba we sett saile thence. This Island will vend som 300:lb of goods in A year but payment must bee most part in provisions which will vend at Pate. But upwards of: 100: [crossed out: or 150] lb worth of Nuckla & Bees wax may bee Annually procured there.

Saileing thence we made ye main land of Mombass & continewed

---

[6] Sandarac, a resin which is obtained from the tree *Callitris quadrivalvis*. It was used in the preparation of varnish and pounce.

coasting for Pate which we discovered with in 48 houers after we sett saile from Pemba being exceedingly helped by A Curentt. & steering in for ye harbour A Pilot boat as accustomary came of [f] to us, wee being with in ye shoules & stering to gett to leeward of A ledg of Rocks to come to an Anchor. But they caused us to come to Anchor wher wee were & tould us ye ground was clere & good. But by woofull experience we found it otherwise, for about midnight our sheat cable was cut & ye Ship drove into shoule water before we could lett fall our best bouer & kedger (being all ye Anchors we had haveing lost our smale bouer at Comero), which brought her up but did not ride [7] her above an houer, for ye Sea went soe high that our basse Cable which was ould & rotten broke midway betwixt ye Ship & ye Anchor. & ye stream Cable cutt in peeces with ye Rocks som what nere ye Anchor, by which time we had bent ye Sheat Cable to a stonn kellak [8] which we made at Johanna, by which weak means it pleased god to preserv us for it rod her till ye Morning. In ye time of our extremity ye Ship strok once A ground driveing over A shole, but blessed bee god tooke noe harme. Assaying in ye Morning to weigh our kellak & stand in to ye harbour. When most of ye Cable was in ye Sea continewing to runn high caused ye Ship to heave ye men from ye Capston & hurt many of them. Wherefore ye men not being able to stand to ye Capston Again, wee bitted ye Cable [put it around the bitts, in order to fasten or slacken it gradually] as short as we could in hopes that some thing would give way, or elce when ye tide came to help us wee must have cut ye Cable. But it pleased god that shortly after, ye straps of ye kellak broke. & we set saile, stood into ye harbour where was good ground & smooth water for ye Ship: rod by one of her gunns. Soe I hasted A shore to procure A great boat to weigh our Sheat Anchor which had a boy [buoy] at it, as none of ye rest had being lett goe in hast, which ye king speedilie furnished us with & seemed very sorowfull for our disaster & not only profering but really indeavouring to supply us with what ye Country afforded that wee wanted. Ye

---

[7] They had dropped their kedge, or small anchor, and the best bower, the anchor carried on the starboard bow; they had already lost the anchor at the port bow. The anchors held the ship only temporarily.

[8] The sheet cable is a hemp cable used when riding in deep water where the weight of a chain cable would strain the bow of the ship. Bending meant that the two ropes were joined together by a bowline knot with the ends made fast upon themselves. The result was not as strong as splicing, but it could be more rapidly done, and also, if necessary, rapidly undone.

Master went in ye boat to weigh ye Anchor with such of our owne people as were able to helpe him & 20: of ye Country people that belonged to ye boat. But there went soe great A sea wher ye Anchor lay that ye boy rope broke [at] ye first Sea that came after they had hould of it before they hove any stresse upon it. Soe wee gave him over for lost being in 10 fadam water. Ye other two Anchors that lay in 4: ffadam: ye people tould us were procurable in calme weather when ye water was clere. They would dive & see for them but [crossed out: being deprived of our anchors] that being uncertain I went to Ampasa A Towne on this Island where ye Portugalls have their residence, A Church & Padre which ye king of Pate will not permit to bee there. But all or most of ye Trade is at Pate, they haveing there 5 saile of Portugall vesells ready to sett saile for Indea being more than usually come hither at other times. Yett have they vended most of their goods though at low prised & Caried thence A great Quantitie of Ivory good part wherof we saw inbarqing at our being at there. The vessells belong 2: to Damon, one to dew, one to Choule & one to Busseene.[9] From ye latter of which I bought an Anchor [costing] 33: Mds. [mahmudis] of that place being about 7C weight which by reason of our necessitie I was forct to buy though at A very dear rate vizt Rys [reis] per Md which Amounts to 66: Rys yett worth it there by reason of ye great price that Iron bears. Ye Ship being at an Anchor again I betooke my selfe to my businesse & treated with ye king of Pate about trade, desireing to draw A Contract with him in writing which hee dearst not doe for feare of ye Portugalls yett promised me fair and curteous usage & assured me for his part to bee free from all kinde of Duties. But the Portugalls tooke Customs of other People that came there. But Capt. Durson [10] at his being there in ye Loyaltie paid them none soe whither we ought to pay it or not hee knew not. Nither would he intermedle with ye businesse on either side but refer

---

[9] Bassein (Basseen), 25 miles north of Bombay, was the seat of the governor who was called the "General of the North." It was captured by the Portuguese in 1536 and was a flourishing port until 1739.

[10] Durson was described as "a most pestiphorus spirit" in O.C. 1986. Durson and Buckeridge were at Mocha in 1650 and probably discussed trade at that time. The *Loyaltie* was a Courten Company ship that carried private goods to Basra and Persia. In 1649 the ship was unable to make its return voyage and had to winter on the coast of Malindi. Its crew at that time consisted of forty Englishmen and a few slaves from Malindi. In 1651 the ship ran aground in the Bay of Bengal and later on the bar at Balasore. The ship was repaired and was used by Durson for his own shipping.

it to ourselves. Wherupon I landed musters of som goods & imployed my selfe in endeavouring their sale and makeing A Cable for ye Ship expecting faire weather to look for our Anchors. But I soone found that there was A Glut of Clothing & ye marchants were all imployed at Ampasa clering Accountts with ye Portugall [crossed out: Shipps] soe that I sould only part of ye Copper & Iron & they at considerable prises. Of ye latter spetie A good Quantity would have vended if we had had it to sell. Ye king of Portugalls factor after their Shipps were dispeeded came to Pate to demaund customs of me, that I tould him that English who had been formerly there paid it not & what we had sould there would hardly suffitien to defray our Charges & what Customs ye former year was taken from us at Mosambiq ye Vice Roy had inordered to bee repaid & that this yeare we paid none at our being there. Nither paid we any customs to them at Congo [11] or other Mores Ports where they toke it of other People. Wherfore I thought it unreasonable to pay it & for A smale matter to bring up A new custom since others had not paid it formerly. Wherfore I would not willingly pay it but refered ye matter to bee determined of betwene ye Vice Roy & yow who better understood it than wee did. Wherupon hee desired me to deposit ye mony into ye king of Pates hands which I would not promise him, but tould him I would advise with ye Master of ye Shipp & give him an Answer. But I heard no more of him save what ye king tould me, that he had been with him to complain & he tould him they & we were both to him as his sonns & hee would not intermedle with ye businesse.

 Haveing finished our Cable & procured A stonne kellak from ye king & wood to make A frame for an other kellak, which if occasion were wee intended to make of A gunne. Ye weather continewing windie & ye working of ye Seas made ye water soe muddy that ye Divers doe noe good in seeking for our Anchors. Ye time of year growing late, & ye Portugall vesells all gonn 10 days before us, we hastened to depart. & before my takeing leave of ye king I desired from him A Letter Unto yow intemating his desires to trade with yow. Which hee refused to doe fearing that ye Portugalls hearing of it might take occasion therby to make wars with him. But tould me I might assure yow that non of our nation should finde from him any worse usage

---

[11] Congo-Bunder, also called Bandar Congo, was a port of some importance for trade on the north shore of the Persian Gulf about 100 miles west of Gombroon, now named Bandar Abbas.

than we & Capt. Durson had already found. But he should bee very glad we would frequent his Porte hopeing that therby the Portugalls Insultacion over him would be mitegated.

 I wrote to yow by ye Damon Ship from Pate adviseing yow in breif what I have here more largly incerted. But being in hast when I wrote it I could not keep its Copie, whefore [*sic*] I cannot remit yow its transcript but desire your excuse.

 The 8th of Sept. wee sett saile from Pate. & being Driven with fresh winds & helped with strong Curents we were soone got to ye Northward of Shockatore [12] & then left to ye expected Calms & litle winds soe wee coveted to gett ye Arabian shore & were gotten by ye 5th [changed from 6] 8obr [October] in 20½ degrees No. Lattitude. & steering easterly for ye Coast of Indea were taken with an extream violent storme. & leying under A Mison [mizzenmast] without any other saile ye force of ye wind pressed ye Ship soe downe that shee lay all along on ye Starbord side with her gunnell [gunwale] in ye water. Her uper works [part of the vessel which is above water level when it is laden for a voyage] being defective & ye waight of our boat soe overpresing our Deck that ye seams opened & ye water ran downe exceedingly, soe much that ye ship had [crossed out: iii, i.e., 3] above 6 foot water in hould at ye after Pump. Wher upon we cut ye Long boat in peeces & hove it over board hopeing that would [crossed out: lighten] righten her & shee would right again. But that being donn & not prevailing wee were fitting to save some of ye riging & cut ye Mainmast by ye board [13] when it pleased god to lay ye wind for ye space of A quarter of an hower soe that ye Ship righted of her selfe & saved her mainmast for that time. But ye wind returning to its former violence we darst not lay ye Ship by again but thought to saile afore it with ye Sprit sail, which imediatly blew from ye yard, when they sett ye foresaile in hopes of better Successe. But that soone followed ye other & blew a way alsoe, soe that we darst loose noe more saile but kept her afore ye wind.[14] Ye storme continewing, ye Sea making a free passage over her waste [and] ye Ship being very deep with ye water

---

[12] Socotra is an island in the Indian Ocean, about 130 miles east of Cape Guardafui. It is 72 miles long and 22 miles wide.
[13] They intended to cut down the mainmast, hoping that the ship would right herself without the weight of the mast.
[14] The wind was blowing so violently that they didn't dare to hold a stationary position with the bow to the wind; they tried to set the bowsprit to sail with it. The bowsprit was blown off and so was the foremast sail when they tried to set it.

ye goods had Sucked up in hould. Our men all tired with pumping & ye water litle or noething abateing, ye Carpenter espied that ye uper wale on ye Starbord side to which ye champlats were fastened was startd & in danger to fley quite out & founder ye Ship, soe that wee were forced to cut our main mast by ye bord.[15] Haveing saved what riging wee could & ye mainyard to make A jure mast. Ye Storme continewing ye 4th day & ye water in hould litle abateing not withstanding our bailing & Pumping abaft. Wee staved [stowed] all our chists betwene decks to make roome for ye Cables to be quoiled in out of ye hould that wee might make A place to baile in ye fore hatch way, when ye tillar of our Ruder broke nere ye rudar head & we were forced to leave of[f] work betwene Decks to mend it again as well as we could & fitt it to steere with takles in ye Gunroome. It being to short to stere with A whip staffe.[16] And that night ye storme decreased & broke up soe that by ye next morning we had faire weather again & by observation at Noone found that wee were under 18 deg: latitude. Ye wind varied in ye time of ye Storme or rather Harecane & blew at times on all Poynts on ye Compas but Most Northwardly which put us back again soe much to ye Southward. I prais God I newer saw ye like & hope I never shall again for ye wind was soe violent that one could scarce looke to windward. & I saw it blow ye ye [sic] lid of[f] A Chest of about 5 foot long out of ye water & end ways turne it above ye water before it fell again. I am hartilie sory it is my unhapinesse to bee ye Author of a Relacion soe sad & tragicall, but since providence hath soe determined, I have learned to be contented with what god either hath or shall send but Shall pray for ye Companys beter successe herafter & in ye interim crave your aceptance of my endeavours though they have in countered such adverce & unexpected successe in the whole tract of ye voyage.

[Buckeridge has crossed out the following: Since ye storme wee have had such smale & adverse winds & Curentts which togither with ye want of our main mast is ye Occasion of our tedious passage. But blessed bee god ye Ship is now safe at an Anchor in Bonbay according to your order, though we intended if ye winds had not hindred us to

---

[15] The carpenter saw that the planks extending along the ship's starboard side in order to strengthen the decks were "started" or loosened by the pressure of the waves; they again decided to cut away the mainmast.

[16] They tried to fasten a whip, or handle, to the tiller, but it was too short; instead they had to steer the ship by tackle in the gunroom.

goe for Damon, by reason that soe much goods aré Damadged & ye Ship soe much out of repaire that much time will be wanting to fitt them for further Disposure for ye goods. It is soe long, wilbe soe long, ere they bee disimbarqued that I feare the greatest part of what are Damadged being two tears of bales wilbe irecurable [irreparable].]

 I had wrote thus much of my Letter shortly after ye storme fearing by reason of our being in soe high a lattitude that I might bee prevented of giveing yow satisfactory advice by our suddame comeing on ye Coast of Indea. But by reason of smale & contrary winds, adverce Curentts, & losse of our Main mast it was ye 19 present before wee made ye land 21 ½ deg: lattitude betwene Cape Gigatt [17] & dio. When sailing with a fair Gaill alongst that shore ye Shipp & goods being soe much damaged, our provisions all spent, haveing had nither bread, buter nor Rork [i.e., pork] for about 20 days before, our Rice all wett & our water halfe mxed with salt water that over floued ye Butts [ends of planks in the ship's side that unite with others in continuing its length] in hould, wee intended if ye winds had favoured us to put over to Rights for Damon hopeing to make ye quicker worke of it & to be nere yow & knowing that there were masts that came from Pate to be procured. But God who doth all for ye best diverted our intentions & sent a fresh easterly wind that put us doune as far as Choule before we made ye land on ye Coast of Indea. Soe wee went according to order for Bombay & blessed be god arived safely there ye 25th Instant, where I received yours of ye 23th Sept. & am Glad yow have received my severall advices though ye import of their contents weere altogeather Sad tydings, yet necesary to bee incerted. & I am glad they have incountred such patient enterteinment, your directions being for our Securitie that we should hasten thence for Buseene or Choule & rather ye former if convenience would admitt. Wee hearing of noe danger to deter us assented to your desires there in being much nerer yow & conveinenter in severall respects.

 I am exceeding joyfull at ye Parliaments victorious Sucesse over ye Dutch therre enemies at home & as sorrowfull for my Masters Losses here. But what is donne by gods permition must bee by us enterteined with patience till hee see fitting to aford redresse which I shall hope, & pray for.

 By ye Inclosed abstracts please to informe your selves what goods I

---

[17] The point of the Kathiawar peninsula, near Dwarka on the Gujarat peninsula. The coast runs from it to Diu without a break.

have sould & what I have brought back that is propper for Sale in Indea. Ye Amount of both being very smale yett could not bee enlarged, therefore I desire my endeavours may be acepted.

The Goods must assuredly bee greatly damadged for there is one teear of bales wet fore & aft & ye 2d tear halfe through. Wherefore it is very necesary the hould were unstoued ye wet Bales taken out, opened, the cloth renched [rinsed] in fresh water, & dreyed, that they may bee in readinesse to be recured if they bee not already past Cure, it being long since they tooke wett. But I shall forbeare to doe anything in it without your order not know whither yow intend we shall stay heare anytime or not. Wherefore I crave & expect your Spedy order therin.

The Ships wants are many which are necessary to bee repaired if you intend to send her a voyage, vizt: A Main Mast & topmast with new riging & blocks for both, alsoe A main stay, new runing riging for all ye other sales, Sale Cloth for a whole sute of Sales, for haveing had much Raine ye Sales & riging are Spoyled, two Anchors and 1 Cable, Some Carpenter worke to put in new knees & stantions [18] to strengthen her uper Deck, & put in A new wale, [and] A new long Boate. Ye Masts may be procured at Damon & ye Corpenters worke both for Ship & boat may bee donne here as reasonable as in Suratt & in probabilitie Cheaper. Anchors may alsoe bee procured here if yow have none in Suratt or else where. But ye Cable riging & Sale Cloth must bee had from Suratt. Seamen are alsoe wanting for we are but 16: English, of which nomber I am one & I feare our nomber wilbe lesned by runawais & mortalitie, haveing some already falne sick. Of these things I presume to advise yow that yow may not bee unacquainted of her condition. If yow have occasion to use her ye Ship is well worth ye repairing, being under water very tight & Strong since ye Storme not makeing an inch of water in A fortnights time. But this reparacion must needs bee chargable & yow haveing other Shipps ready fitted, I beleive, yow will rather Chuse to lay her up then, then not haveing except your new Supplys have brought them, men enough to man them.

[The following has been crossed out: I shall yett presume further

---

[18] The knees were crooked pieces of timber, having two branches or arms, used to connect the beams of a ship with her sides; one branch to the deck beam, the other to a timber of the ship's side. The stanchions were small pillars of wood or iron, used for supporting the decks.

to propound to yow A voyage: if yow shall aprove therof, for Mombasso & Mosambiq, to both which places A Ship may well goe that leaving ye Coast of Indea in June & touch at Johanna on ye back sid of ye island by the way to leave your Letters for ye outer bound Ships [two words undecipherable] with whom shee may Joyne for such further Service as yow shall in order in her returne but herof it is reque]

If yow intend another voyage for the coast Melinde with ye goods we have, Mombasse & Mosambiq are ye best ports, as ye case now stands with us, for both which places our goods are proper & ye part that is proper for one porte are improper for ye other. It is requisite yow treat with ye viceroy for license & order to bee freed from or favoured in ye Customs which is ye Cheif reason of my forwardnesse in adviseing yow herof, for by this means ye Company may bee rid of their goods which we have here which will not otherwise conveniently bee. I humblie crave your ffavurable Sensure of my forwardnesse herin & shall readylie submit both my selfe & opinion to your better Judgments.

Bombay affording noe Cossetts [couriers] to transport my Letter towards yow, nither haveing any acquaintance in Busseene to recomend ye Businesse unto, I hasted thence ye next day after we came thither & have had a longer passage than expected to this place. But god bee thanked ye Shipp is now safe at an Anchor without ye Barr of Busseene. & we intend god willing to bring her in to Morrow when wee can gett of A Pilot. Thus with ye Due tender of my humble & harty service to your acceptance, I obsequeously subscribe.

Buss: 9mbr [November] 30th   your observant servant
1653   N B

XVI

The following letter, written to the president at Surat, breaks off abruptly and seems to be incomplete. Evidently strong complaints had been registered against Buckeridge and his crew for the unprofitable voyage they had just completed. In his letter Buckeridge condemns Jeremy Raymond, the master of the *Assada Merchant*, placing the blame for the failure entirely on him. Several signs of disagreement between the two appear in Buckeridge's earlier letters and reports. Raymond, as master, was to have obeyed the orders of Nicholas Buckeridge; see Appendix B for a transcript of the instructions given to Raymond for the voyage.

Worshipfull & Worthy ffriends

    Since you are displeased at my returne for Indea on ye Pinnace Assada Marchant with her Cargo undisposed of, which tends to ye Companys great losse by reason of ye Damage that hath hapned thereto by ye way, I crave your perusall herof for further Sattisffaction therin. It being my desires herby to acquaint yow ye reasons that induced me thereto, which were Cheiflie occasioned by ye aversenesse & backwardnesse of Jeremy Raymond Comaunder of ye said Pinnace. Yett since I esteeme not A Generall accusation Suffitientlie Satisfactorie I shall instance some particular Circumstances for your ffurther Sattisffaction.
    ffindeing his desirs in ye tearme of our outward bound Passage much inclined to goe to Mosambiq, pretending that to bee A place hee knew & was confident of his goeing to it (but rather meaning if I missensure not, to dispose of A parcell of Almonds hee had in ye Shipp, wher on he there expected exterordenary profitt and conceived them to bee elce where unvendable). I laboured to disswade him from it by acquainting him how we were designed & forbid to goe under Comaund & would not assent unto what he propounded though hee brought us in sight of Mosambiq but oposed him & Caused him to pass by and prosecute his voyage for Sena, which hee did though very unwillinglie. For being by ye way once gott to an Anchor under ye Islands of Angosas he made som slight pretenses grounded on ffears

Worsp: & worthy ffriends

Since you are dissatisfied at my
returne for India on ye Lennard Affr a
ndrt: wth her Cargo: and disposd of wth
tends to ys Compa: great losse by reason
of ye Damage ye Salt Raymond thereby
ys way I rec..d ye Psalts best for farther
satisfaction therein it being my desire
Rely to acqt yor: yr reasons yt induce
me thereto, wth were this I let one finde
by ye adversenesse & backwardnesse of
Jeremy Raymond Comaunder of ye said
Lennard yott: fride I esteeme not a Small ayrse-
tion Sufficiently Satisfactoryd
I shall in same some Pticuler Circum-
stances for ye further Satisfaction —
finding his desire in ye tearme of
D: outward bou.. Passage much inclined
to goe to Mosaimbiq: ye tending of to bee
A place hee knew () was conseitd of his
goeing to it (but wather meaning if J
misfortune not to dispose of A Psell of
Almonds hee ha.. in ye Shipp where on he
thare opposed outward oudery psell and
woud desyre onward ym to bee els where londinde
forbid to goe. (for) I laboured to disswade him from it
under Comaund woud not off sent unto ye thoyh

and suppositions, & trifled away some time there needleslie, till very faire winds & weather made him Ashamed to stay there any longer. Hee venterd thence and soone after meeting with A storme he took occasion therby to disswade me from farther prosecution of ye voyag, pretending A ffeare to bee imbayed & that ye Shipp might force out her Bous by rideing at An Anchor if such an other storme should befall us & would faine have had my Consent to leave that Coast & goe away either for Augustine Bay or Mosambiq. But findeing that hee could not prevaile with me when ye storme broke up, hee contineued his Cource for Sena, but still kept A great distance from ye Shore, Anchored in Depe water, & would not bee perswaded to Anchor in lesse than 7 fadam water & at least 7 miles of [f] of ye shore. Wherat I intimated my dislike in regaurd of the great Routh to ye shore but could not disswade him, hee telling me ye President had trusted him with his shipp & hee would cary her to him in safety.

Haveing been at Sena & finding that hee would not venture to cary ye Ship into ye River without A Pilot from ye Shore which could not bee procured, I urged him to proceede for Ingumbane, which hee did though unwillinglie reiterating his former desirs to leave that coast. And being come nere to that place & at An Anchor ye wind freshening hee weighed & stood away to ye Southward without asking my consent or advice therein. & being passed that & there alsoe frusterated I still urged his continuing for Cape Corintas & further for ye Bay of Lorenso Marqs & assembled all ye Ships officers for their advice concerning it. When perceiveing hee could not yett prevaile with me hee burst out into passionate expressions, saying if hee must goe hee must goe [a] happie man; bee his dole hee should fare as well as ye rest. Yett on further Consideracion hee resolved not to goe to ye Southward of Cape Corintas. Nither could I perswade him to come againe on ye Coast in quest of ye Port of Ingumbane. After wee were forced to beare up by reason of A Southerly Storme that forced us to Leeward of ye Shoules of ye Jews leying in about 22d So. latitude betwene ye Maine & ye Island of St. Laurence soe that wee could not goe to Augustine Bay but bore up for Mosambiq. And after we had been at Mosambiq & came thence for ye Island of Johanna [crossed out: & after ye needlesse expence of many] spent days there, hee was very unwilling to goe thence (though I had there procured A Pilot) saying hee would not intrust ye Ship into A Black Rogues hands. Yett after A sharpe Contention I prevailed with him but not without much grudging & exclaiming against ye Company, for his smale salary & exacting soe much for mony paid him here, saying he was noething beehoulding to them, & but under valued his imployment saying hee had rather bee A Mate in an: other Ship than Master in this, & was this A Voyage to send A man on ye ffirst time hee was Master & many such expressions to tedious to incert.

And being by Gods mercy preserved from very imenent dangers and arived in safety at Pate, finding ye very Civill & Curteous & ye Place of Porte of Considerable trafiq though then Glutted, I propounded our stay there unto him, which hee would not agree unto saying that by reason wee were not inordered soe to doe. If it hapned well it would bee well taken, but if otherwise ye blame would bee imputed to us. Which I assured him hee need not to feare and used many arguments to perswade him, but could not prevaile. Soe that being quite tired with his Crosseness, backwardnesse, drunkennesse, & abusivenesse (And findeing som reason for his last unwilingnesse because wee had lost all our Anchors & Consequently unprovided to goe for other places wher good ground takle is very requisite, without goeing to which places wee could not dispose of our goods, very litle of them being proper for Pate) I yeilded to our comeing for Indea.

And after our arivall to Bassene & had received your Answer to my Letter wherin yow intemated your dislike at our returne, I acquainted him therwith, when hee seemed to Justifie himselfe. But being Convicted ye next Morning hee came to me Privatlie & intreated me soe to excuse ye matter that ye ffault might not be imputed to him, saying hee was A Pore man & ye Company might stopp his wages and uterly undoe him, which I deneyed, & tould him I must acquaint ye President & Councell with ye truth of ye matter & lett him excuse it to them as well as he could. When finding hee could not prevaile with me hee shortly after tooke occasion to quarell with me & in his drinke much to abuse me A [sic] because I would not consent to his makeing new Bulk heads & grateings in ye Shipp contending it needlesse. Hee affirmed that it must bee donne & if I would not allow ye doeing it lett ye Dutch take her & ye Divell goe wither.

ffinis

XVII

This letter was written several years after the preceding; Buckeridge is now a merchant in London. The persons mentioned in the letter, unfortunately, could not be identified. Perhaps the "Mr. Wilde" is Charles Wylde, author of the "Journal of the Ship Bonitto" mentioned above.

My Honoured Good ffriend
Capt. Robt. Stringer

I have received your severall Letters by some & Copies by other Shipps that came this yeare from St. Helena by which I perceive your Government Distracted & yow discontent at ye Companys soe Easie Crediting ffalce Reports, but better is not to be Expected. I hartilie wish you safely returned to your Native Countrey & well clere of them, but that will scarcely bee without some trouble. Your kinde tokens by Mr. Deverell are Safely & thankfully received as is ye Pott of Civett yow sent by him, alsoe ye Glasse of Civett by Mr. Goodyar & ye Civett & Topaz by Mr. Wilde, to whome I paid 11 lb as you desired. But I have not yett sould any of your Civett, but shall endeavour ye sale of it soe soone as I can. Your Topaz, as you call it, is of smale value & shalbe reserved for yow or your Order. Ye best way to dispose of it wilbe to cutt it out into smale stones, & hapilie I may make A treyall of A smale peece of it. If these hapen to come to you at St. Hellena let me desire yow to bring or send me 2 or 3 of your young shee Goats for I have A great fancy to them & shall thankfully allow yow ye value of them. And wishing all health & hapinesse to your selfe, your good Lady & ffamily I Cordially Conclude

Your realy affectionate ffriend & Servant
London ffebr ye 18th anno 1669   Nicho. Buckeridge

XVIII

This final note penned by B. B. — Bainbridge Buckeridge, son of Nicholas Buckeridge — causes some speculation. Perhaps the "Letters upon Severall occasions" which do not follow are reposing unidentified in a library somewhere. Perhaps one can also assume that this is the year in which Buckeridge died, his son having assembled his papers at that time.

Finis

ye end of my Fathers Letters in this book

B B.

1689

Coppys of Lres upon Severall occasions follow —

Appendixes

Appendix A

Commission & Instructions given by us the President and Councell of India, Persia, Etc unto Mr. Nico. Buckeridg, bound to Cape Corinthes: Coast of Suffola, Mozambiq and Millinda.

Our Loveing Friend Mr. Nicholas Buckridge

    By the encouragedment we have received from yow by what you relate unto us of a hopefull and beneficiall trade, that is to bee procured about Cape Corinthes and other places upon the Coast of Suffola, Mozambiq and Millinda which being once thoroughly discovered may with the Assistance of the Almighty prove very advantagious unto our honnourable Employers, wee are inducd once more, to make triall of what it shall please ye Lord to make you Instrumentall in the discovery of those parts, to the Glory of his name the honnour of our Nacon and benefite of our said Employers, and for that purpose wee have caused theire pinnace Assada to bee trimmed victualed & monied and laden aboard her a Cargazoon of goods to the import according to Invoyce delivered yow on which Shipp we now have you take Your passage and as winde, and Weather shall permitt sale unto ye Cape Corinthes or any port or place thereabouts, or to any port or place upon ye Coast of Suffola Millinda or Mozambiq and theire to discover, sell barter or Exchange what goods soever you have on board for account of the Honnourable Company with what people soever you shall encounter & for what Comodities you shall find amongst them as Gold, Elliphants teeth, etc which you know may bee for theire advantage and which ye same with what Conveniente speed you may returne to the port of Suratt, to render an account to us the President and Councell of what you have effected in this same voiage.

    And be cause we would not have ye hopefull designe in any way to bee prejudiced by our Strickt Injunction wee have left you free to goe to what port or place in the above named parts you thinke good, and to Trade, with what kinde of people soever you shall there finde, and have likewise ordered the Master of the said pinnace Assada, to follow your order, in saleing to Such ports as you Shall advise and there to stay untill you shall order his departure and soe from port to port as you Shall have occation to direct and the shipp may safely come, but with all we advise yow not to Come under Comannd of any portugalls ffortification or trust yourselves with them more then necessity Requires, neither part with any of your goods till you have Satisffacion for it or well Secured to have it at Such a time as you agree as within 4: or 5 daies, or ye Like but wee would not have yow in any place permit of goods, to bee paid the next yeare or when you shall Returne thither againe dispose of anithing, other then for present Satisfacon, but rather returne ye goods agaaine upon the Shipp with you.

Wee would alsoe often have yow Consult with Mr Richard Aston (whome we appoint your Second and is [i.e., in] case of Mortallity is to Succeede yow and with Mr. Jeremy Raymond the Master about your intended designe, and Communicate of your intencons Concerning the said voiage as in Case of your mortality (which God fore the said Mr. Aston may bee able to act Something for the benefite of our Honnourable Employers which said Mr Aston wee Constitute, and appoint in your Steede, for the disp[eeding] and ordering of all thinges in thy present voiage for our Masters Advantage and in such case wee joine Mr. Jer. Raymond in Committee with Mr Aston without whose Consent he to act anything in ye Companies Affaires, in such Case he is to make use, and as neare as may bee ffollow this our Commission.

And though wee have not appointed yow a Sett time when with ye assistance of the Almighty yow shall Returne yet wee desire yow if possible you would soe order your Businesse, that yow might bee with us againe some tyme in October at farthest and let it not bee a small occation, that may Cause your longer stay for if the Businesse prove beneficiall yow may the sooner Returne againe if otherwise your longer stay will but bring the greater Losse (and wee hope ye Best).

Yet for your more Security as the State of Affaires now stand betweene us and the Dutch, wee would have yow to order your Businesse, that yow may come to Augustine Bay, before ye arrivall of any of the Europe Shippes that by them you, may bee informed whither wee have warre or peace with the dutch, and accordingly order your selfe if you finde wee have peace, and they come soe timely, that yow may gaine ye Cape of Guardifiw by the 5th or 10th August then yow are to hasten thither and [undeciphered word] your Selves to passe in the mouth of the Gulph, that you may bee ready to surprise any vessell belonging to Decan that hath not our passe, wee

Send by yow a letter to ye Comaunder of such Shipps, as shall Come, out of Europe to that purpose, and for what money treasure or rich Comodities they have on board let it bee seized on for ye Companys use and lett the vessell goe again giveing them a receipt for what money yow take from them, and take a noate from them, how much it is alsoe, not Suffering anithing to be taken from them, but what yow Shall register, but in case you Should meete with noe Europe Shippes, either there or at Johanna before ye 20th August nor by other meanes be advised that wee have peace with the duch, then endeavor to gaine ye Coast of India and goe into Bom bay and there remaine in Case of warres with the duch, till further order from us, You have for your Assistant, Mr. John Mudjatt, a Servant of the Company as you finde him Capable, and delligent, you may employ him, but wee would have yow Instruct, and advise him, in what you see him wanting, in that hee may bee the better able to doe the Companys good Service hereafter.

There is alsoe Mr. [undeciphered name] that Came upon ye Assada desirige to accompany yow in this voiage, to which wee have Condiscended and given him Licence to Carry with him two small Bales of paupes, with this promise, that hee deliver them into your hands to dispose of and not to make Sale of them, untill Such Goods as yow have of the Companys bee first put if you will finde him a Rationall man and one that will stand yow in some steede upon occation the Consideracon whereof induceth us to Licence him to voiage with yow.

The Like Care, you are to take of any other Goodes, that are upon ye Shipp, to whomesoever they belong, that you suffer not any man to dispose of ought, untill you have first made sale of that belongeth, to ye Company and then if they have any small matter, amongst them, let them in ye name of God make the best of it, but see you soe order the sale of it, for them, that they spoile not ye trade, wee hope to have in the ffuture soe hoping your Endeavoures wilbe noe way wanting in the Improvement of this designe to ye most advantage, Wee Committ you to the protection of the Almighty, praying for his Blessing upon these your undertakeinges and a safe Returne unto,

Swally Marrine ye 12th December 1652   Your Loving freinds
                                                                             Jer Blackman
                                                                             Jn: Pearce
                                                                             Geo: Oxinden
                                                                             Tho: Breton

[Legend on the outside: Commission to bee observed by Mr. Nicholas Buckeridge dated the 12th December 1652.]

Appendix B

Comissions & Instructions Given by us ye President and Councell of India Persia Etc. unto Mr Jeremy Rayman Master of Pinnace Assada Merchant bound from ye Road, unto Cape Corinthes, Coast of Soffola, Mussambique Melinde & soe back unto Swally Road whether the Almighty Conduct him

Our Loveing ffriend Mr Jeremy Rayman

You are with the first fair winds and tyde, after you have received on board Mr Nicholas Buckeridge, Richard Aston, John Mudgett, sett saile, & as wind, tyde and weather will permitt, sale for ye Cape of Corinthes, or such port or places thereabouts, as Mr. Nicho. Buckeridge your Cape merchant shall appoint, & there to stay untill he shall order your departure & from thence alongst the Coast of Soffola Mussambique and Melinda & to any port or place therein as he shall Direct you, & the ship may safely come, & from thence with the assistance of the Almighty retourne to Surratt againe In all which time of the voyadge, we desire you to ffollow ye order & direction of ye said Mr Buckeredge to what ports you shall sale, & not to depart thence till he shall order the same likewise, & alwayes to be ayding & assisting him with boates & men in lading and unlading your said Ship & in what elce he shall desire, conducing to the Benifitt of our Honourable inployers in your present designe till it shall please ye Almighty to retourne unto us in safety.

Wee beleeve ye Injuries ye Company have suffered by ye King of Vizapoore in seazing of their Cloth in anno 1648 at Rajapore & other considerable damages is not unknowne unto you as that likewise what payne and Endeavours have bin used in a fayre way, to procure satisfaction from them but all in vayne, so that there is nothing now remaynes but to force them to doe us Justice, which by entreatyes they have so long refused to doe, these are therefore in ye name of our honourable Imployers to require you to use the utmost of your endeavours either by force or faire meanes to make stay of, seaze on for their use, all such ships and vesells as belong to any port of ye King of Vissapore (which is from Goa & Choule) not haveing our passes, that you shall upon ye seas encounter with & such ship or vessell so taken or seized you are to take an exact account of all such goodes & Merchandizes that shall be found aboard them, & suffer nothing thereof to be perloyned but kept intire untill you retourne to us, if you meet with them outward bound and ye like till you come to Surratt if you encounter them in your retourne, but ye people of all such vessells, we would have used with all Courtesie, & if they resist, not to shed in blood, we would not have them plundered of anything that belongeth to them, & if you encounter any vessels that hath Persians therein, you must very carefull they be not ronged in the least, least we suffer for it at Gombroone, And for all places where you come or persons that you meete with, all such shall be herein concerned, you are to lett them know, what endeavours have for three yeares been used, to gett satisfaction by faire meanes, both at court with the king, & at Rajapore where ye President himselfe went last yeare, purposely in afaire way to compose this difference, but all proved fruitlesse, soe that we are necessitated to use this force which we shall againe forbeare when we have obteyned satisfaction for our damiges and assurance of better dealing in the future, & for the better encouredgment of your people to be diligent in assisting in this businesse, if you come to engage you may promise them one six part of what they soe take & we will see it made good unto them, provided they abuse not ye Company or people in perloyning ought from them, and soe you may acquaint them.

 All businesse of consequence shall be determined by consultation, where Mr Buckeridge your selfe & such officers, as are usually convented shall voat & act according to ye desert of the offender.

 Our former Commissions have laide forth our requiers soe amply about seizing of Mallabers that we refer you to the perusall thereof.

 If in the Voyadge you are now designed on, it should please the Lord to take you of this life (which God forbid, we then appoint your cheife mate Joseph Collins to be your successor unto him we require the Company to be obedient as to you their present Master and soe ye almighty prosper you, in your designe and send you safe and seasonable passage and safe retourne unto,

Swally Mareen ye 12 December 1652	Your loving ffreinds Jeremy Blackman Edward Pearce George Oxinden Thomas Bretton

P.S. You know upon what uncertaine termes the Dutch & we stand, therefore we require you to be carefull how you trust to them, or any Christian vessells you meete with in the Sea, unlesse they be such, as belong unto the Company nor suffer your selves, by any friendly invitacon to be drawne out of your ship, for ye tymes are soe dangerous, we know not, whoe are our freinds and in these respects pray lett your ship be alway in readiness to repell any that shall assault you, and if you meete with any French vessell, either at sea or at port above all trust them nott, for you may be sure, they come for noe good.

And to what port soever you come unto, we require you to be carefull, you send noe more, of your company on shoare, then is requisite, and if you come to a place which you any way doubt of, lett them not goe on shoare unarmed, & we would have you very cautios how you leave your ship and be alwayes ready to resist any if may probably appeare to be your enimies.

[Labeled on the outside: Comission for Mr. Jeremy Rayman, December 12th 1652.]

Index

Index

Abex, coast of. *See* Malindi, coast of
Achin, 8
Aden, governor of, 4
Africa, East: dangerous coast, 46, 51; first voyage to, 6, 19; second voyage to, 11; trade, 7
Agra, 9, 24n
Ahmadabad, 9, 41
Almonds, 24, 82
Ambergris: at Delagoa Bay, 42, 54; at Inhambane, 32, 43, 66; at Inhaqua Island, 66; at Masseluge, 31; at Pate, 45; at Sofala, 32; mentioned, 7
"Amboina Massacre," 8–9
Ampasa, 38, 46, 75, 76
Angola, 22
Angosa, Islands of (Ilha Angoche), 60, 82
Arab traders, 6
Ashmore, Michael, 36
Assada Island (Nossi Bé): beef from, 31; Courten Company colony at, 10, 19, 58n, 67n; maps of, 22n; merchants to, 67; Portuguese ship to, seized, 21; slaves from, 46; trade goods from, 46, 57, 65; trade with Mozambique, 44; trade with Pate, 46; Wylde manuscript about, 22n
Assada Merchant: accused of spying, 64; and Buckeridge, 6; cargo capacity, 20; crewmen injured, 74; crew's illnesses, 65, 66, 73, 80; damage to, 77–78; description, 19–20; drifts off anchorage, 60, 61, 74; lack of provisions, 79; readied for voyage to Africa, 91; repairs needed, 74, 80; returns with cargo unsold, 82; to Batticaloa, 11, 47; to Cambodia, 12; to Madagascar and East Africa, 19; to Mozambique, 11; used to colonize Assada, 10; mentioned, 35, 48, 49, 56, 68, 93
Aston, Richard: death of, 58, 65; to succeed Buckeridge, 92; mentioned, 51, 52, 94
Augustine Bay: compared to Dartmouth, England, 48; counterfeiting by Courten Company at, 67; Courten Company colony at, 10; letters to be left at, 19, 49, 61, 68; letters to be picked up at, 92; mentioned, 56, 57, 60, 63, 84
Austin (crewman), 52

Bainbridge, Sarah, 14
Bainbridge, William, 14
Bainbridge Street, 15
Bajun Islands, 72n
Baker, Aaron, 50
Baker, Mrs., 50
Balasore, 75
Banda Islands, 40
Bandar Abbas (Gombroon), 12, 58n, 59n, 76n
Bank of England, 16
Bantam, 4, 8, 11, 40, 50n, 58n
Basra (Bussora), 3, 19, 40, 52, 58n, 59n, 75n
Bassas da India (Baxos da India, Shoals of India, Shoules of ye Jews, Baxios de Judia) 57, 63, 84
Bassein (Basseen, Bussene, Basein), 70, 75, 79, 81, 85
Batavia, 12
Batticaloa, 11, 47
Beads, 7, 32, 42, 54
Beeswax, 7, 44, 45, 73
Bengal, 9, 40, 50n
Bengal, Bay of, 75n
Betel nuts, 47
Bijapur, 67n
Blackman, Jeremy, 47, 56, 93, 95
Blaeu, Joan, 22n
Bodleian Library, Oxford, 16, 47
Bombay, 78, 79, 81, 93, 75n
Bonito, 22n, 86
Bostock, James, 40
Bourne, William, 15
Brass, 32
Brava (Braba), 35, 37, 46
Brazil, 7
Bread, 30
Breton, Francis, 3
Bretton, Thomas, 47, 93, 95
Broach, 9, 40
Browne, William (boatswain), 58, 65

Buckeridge, Arthur, 3
Buckeridge, Bainbridge, 15, 16, 87
Buckeridge, Elizabeth, 15
Buckeridge, Jane, 15
Buckeridge, John, 3
Buckeridge, Nicholas: biography of, 3, 4, 6, 12, 15, 87; called spy, 65; commission for, 91–93; company service, 4, 6, 11, 12, 14, 94; company's instructions to, 6, 10, 12, 14, 91–93, 95; and Courts of Committee meetings, 12, 14; diplomatic relations of, 23, 26, 28, 29, 30, 57, 63, 70; disputes with Jeremy Raymond, 82–85, John Totty, 5, others in company, 11; and Dutch and English War, 11, 79; journal and letter book of, 16; letters from, 34, 56, 48, 68, 86, 87; manuscripts of, 16, 47; provided with provisions at Mkoani, 34; receives letters or gifts, 21, 26, 35, 79; recommends ship be sent to East Africa, 91; recommends trade goods, 12; returns to England, 12, 14; sends gifts, 27, 34, 35; settlements by Company in favor of, 14; urged by king to help in local war, 72; warned not to steal customs, 28
Buckeridge, Nicholas (relative), 3
Buckeridge, Sarah (daughter), 15
Buckeridge, Sarah (wife), 14
Buckeridge Street, 14–15
Burgone Island, 38
Bury cum Hepmangrove, 15
Butter, 35
Bynge (crewman), 53

Cabreira, Francisco de Seixas, 71n, 72
Cairato, Joao Batista, 45
Cambay, 29n, 44
Cambay, Gulf of, 40n
Cambodia, 12
Cane, 53
Carrying trade, 6–7
Cartwright, Ralph, 50n
Cauche, François, 22n
Ceylon, 7, 11
Chaul (Chowle, Chaoul, Choule), 21, 28, 44, 58, 75, 79, 94
Cheese, 24, 53
Chefina do Meio Island, 33n
Chefina Grande Island, 33n
Chefina Pequena Island, 33n
China, 7
Cinnamon, 7, 50n

Civet, 45, 86
Cloth: damaged en route, 4, 11, 79, 80; described, 9; piece goods, 50n; sources of supply, 9; adgrees, 52; baftas, 31n, 40, 41, 55; besutos, 55; bezan, 55; brawles, 31, 41, 44, 54; byrampauts (beiramee, byramee, byrams), 24n, 25, 27, 31, 40, 41, 52, 53, 54, 55, 93; calico, 7, 42, 43, 44, 45; cannequin (cannikeen), 30, 31; chabnam (rosee), 55; chautar (chaw), 55; chintz, 41, 52; deribands, 52; dutties, 32, 52; guzzy baftas, 31; palempore, 52, 69; pautkas, 32; salloos, 41, 52; satin, 40; silk, 7; soosy, 69; tappichindaes, 41; turban, 41n; veneas, 27, 31
Cloves, 8
Cockayne, William, 4
Coconut, 30
Cocteens, Jacinta, 64
Coins: crusado (xado), 24n; mamudi (Ma., Mds., Ms.), 32; pardao (pardo), 22n; rial of eight, 31; rupee (rups), 52; xerafine (sherateen), 71
Collins, Joseph, 95
Comoro Islands (Comero), 10, 44n, 50, 60, 74
Congo Bunder, 76
Copper, 32, 76
Corintas, Cape, 32, 42, 48, 49, 51, 60, 63, 84, 91, 94
Coromandel, 7, 9, 49
Cosmoledo Islands, 59
Courten, William, 10
Courten, William (son), 10
Courten Company: abolished and combined with United Joint Stock Company, 10; counterfeiting at Augustine Bay, 10, 67; mentioned, 75n. *See also* Assada Island
Cranmer, Robert, 3
Cross, Joseph, 4
Currents, 34, 49, 51n, 57, 59, 63, 71, 73

Dahlak Island (Delieka), 4
Damanganga River, 23n
Damon (Daman, Damão): ship from, 23, 75, 77; mentioned, 36, 79, 80
Dartmouth, 48
Decan, ship from, 67, 93
Delagoa Bay, 32, 42, 54, 63, 84. *See also* Inhaqua Island
Deverell, Mr., 86
Diu (Dew, Dio, Due): described, 26;

merchants, 28; ships from, 30, 57, 65, 75; mentioned, 22n, 44, 59, 79
Dove, 52
Durson, Capt., 75, 77
Dutch and English war: news on to be received at Augustine Bay, 92; in Persian Gulf, 11, 50n, 52, 59n; requests for information on, 49, 68; at Surat, 10, 68; treaty signed, 11; uncertainty about, 96
Dwarka, 79n
Dyott, Simon, 14
Dyott Street, 14, 15

East India Company. *See* English East India Company
Ebony, 30
Elizabeth I, 8
English East India Company: administration of, 3–4; and Assada survivors, 10; and Courten Company, 10; Courts of Committee meetings, 12, 14; and Dutch, 8, 12; early history, 7–10; factories at Achin, 8, at Agra, 9, at Ahmadabad, 9, at Broach, 9, 40n, at Surat, 9, 23n, in Cambodia, 12; letter to Mozambique, 21; loss of ships, 11, 50n; policy toward booty, 94; policy toward private trade, 93; and Portuguese, 9; trade at Aden, 5, at Bantam, 12, in East Indian Archipelago, 9, in India and Indian Ocean, 9, with Persia, 9

Falcon, 52n, 59
Falmouth, 50n
Faza, 38
Flacourt, Étienne de, 22n
Fort Jesus, 45n, 72n
Fort St. George, 40, 50n
Francis, 4, 29
Fruit, 30, 35

Gama, Vasco da, 6, 36n, 38n
Garway, William, 12
Gigatt, Cape, 79
Gloves, 53
Goa: bills of exchange in, 57; customs of, 28, 29; merchants from, 28; rice from, 30; ships from, 23, 30, 44, 57, 65, 94; wheat from, 30
Goats, 86
Gold: gold dust, 43; gold mines, 31; at Malindi, 39n; as payment, 28, 29; at Sena, 32, 44; mentioned, 7, 91
Gombroon. *See* Bandar Abbas

Good Hope, Cape of, 7
Goodyear, John, 53
Goodyear, Mr., 86
Gosse (crewman), 23, 24
Griffin, Roger, 52, 59n
Guardafui, Cape, 77n, 92
Gujarat peninsula, 7, 9, 26n, 41, 79n

Happy Entrance, 14
Hinde, 40, 52n
Horses, 7
Hugos. *See* Iungo River
Hunt, Robert, 10, 67
Hunter, John (gunner's mate), 58, 64, 65

Illness: of Buckeridge, 4; of crew, 64, 65, 66, 73, 80; of governor of Mozambique, 57, 64, 65; mentioned, 6
Incomati River, 32
Indigo, 50n
Inhambane (Ingombane), 32, 43, 54, 56, 60, 62, 63, 65, 66, 84
Inhaqua Island, 66
Interlopers, 8. *See also* Courten Company
Iron, 44, 45, 76
Iungo River, 36n
Ivory (Elliphants teeth): at Delagoa Bay, 42, 54; duty on, 28; at Inhambane, 32, 43, 66; at Inhaqua Island, 66; at Malindi, 39n; at Mozambique, 24, 25, 27, 28, 30, 32, 44, 72, 73; at Pate, 45, 75; at Quelimane, 43; at Quiloa, 44, 71; at Seefa River, 62; at Sena, 31, 43; at Sofala, 32; at Zanzibar, 73; mentioned, 7, 91
Ivory, hippopotamus (seahorse teeth), 32

James I, 8
James, 67
James Ford Bell Library, 22n
Japan, 7
Jesuit priest, 25, 27
Joan, Vincente, 26
Johanna (Joh:, Johana, Joanna): letters left at, 60, 70, 81; trade with Mozambique, 44; mentioned, 49, 51, 55, 56, 57, 59, 60, 67, 68, 74, 84, 93
Juan de Nova (St. Johns), 37n, 50n

Kathiawar peninsula, 79n
Knives, 53

Lanneret, 6, 50n
Lead, 46
Lemons, 30

Levant Company, 7, 8
Lima, Francisco de, 53
Lisbon, ship from, 22
Lourenço Marques, 54
Love, 50
Loyaltie, 75
Lualua River, 61
Lucknow, 24n

Madagascar. *See* St. Lawrence
Madras, 4, 14, 40, 50n
Madraspatam, 22n
Mafia (Monfia), 33, 55
Magadoxa (Mogadishu, Mogadiscio), 35, 36, 46
Magincate River, 20n
Makassar, 11
Makongwe Island, 34
Malabar, 5, 7, 95
Malindi (Malinda, Malinde), 6, 38, 91, 94
Malindi, coast of, 36, 48, 59, 68
Manica gold field, 31n
Maputa River, 33
Marmalade, 53
Mashona gold field, 31n
Massawa (Mussora), 4
Masseluge (Masselage), 31, 44, 46
Massey, Jonathan, 40
Massey, Walter, 40
Masulipatam, 40, 49n, 50n
Matola River, 33
May, Matthew, 15
Maynard, William, 14
Maynard Street, 15
Meat: beef, 30, 31, 35; hens, 30, 35; mutton, 30
Merca (Morca), 46, 66
Merchants: of Muscat, 69; of Pate, 69
Milk, 35
Millet, 7
Mkoani, 34, 35
Mocha (Maccoa), 4, 6, 19, 30, 75n
Moluccas, 7, 9
Mombasa (Mombass, Bombass, Bombasse, Mombasse), 36, 38, 45, 71, 73, 81
Mombasa, governor of: trade to Quiloa, 44; trade to Sena, 43, 44; mentioned, 33n, 71, 72
Monsoons, loss of, 22
Moors, 54
Mosse (counterfeiter), 67
Mottingham, 3
Mozambique: anchorage, 20; Buckeridge advises voyage to, 81; climate, 43, 65; description, 30; fort at, 20, 43; goods sold at, 23, 55, 57; king's factor at, 28, 53; provisions, 30, 43, 72; ship arrivals, 65; town ruined by king of Pemba's soldiers, 71; mentioned, 61, 63, 68, 82, 84, 91, 94
Mozambique, governor of: angry with Buckeridge, 27, 63; controls Portuguese ships going to Sena, 31; councils with his merchants, 21; delays payment, 27, 57; entertains Buckeridge, 57; gifts for, 24, 53; gifts from, 26, 29; illness of, 57, 64, 65; permits unloading, 27; promises no duties to be paid, 25; refuses request for house, 23, 25; regulates prices for trade, 66; requires musters, 23; sends his priest to confer with Jesuit, 26; ship from Sena, 27, 65; trade at Delagoa Bay, 42; trade at Inhambane, 43
Mudgett, John, 93, 94
Muscat, Arabs from, 46, 72, 73

Narbada River, 40n
Navigation Act of *1651*, 10
Nazarite, 22
Negapatam, 49n
Nokes, William, 40

Olive oil, 53
Olives, 53
Oman, Gulf of, 72n
Oranges, 30
Orme, John, 52, 53
Oxinden, George, 47, 93, 95

Page, Thomas, 67
Parak, Tulsi Das Khan, 40
Pate (Patta): customs duty demanded, 76; described, 34; Portuguese trade at, 45; provisions to be sold at, 73; trade to Masseluge and Assada, 46; mentioned, 38, 48, 49, 59, 66, 68, 74, 77, 85
Pate, king of, 75, 76
Pearce, Edward, 47, 93, 95
Pemba, 33, 45, 55, 66, 70, 71, 73
Pepper, 7
Persia, 9, 19, 75n
Pistachio nuts, 53
Portugal: annexation by Spain, 7; and trade in Indian Ocean, 6, 7, 42
Portuguese and English war, 49
Portuguese empire, 7
Prisoners of war, 72

Provisions, lack of, 79
Prows, 30

Quelimane, 43, 61, 62
Quiloa, 44, 45, 55, 70

Rajapore, 94, 95
Raymond, Jeremy (master): accompanies Buckeridge to governor of Mozambique, 29; Buckeridge's letter to, 48; cautioned regarding landing and leaving ship, 96; commission for, 94–96; criticized by Buckeridge, 82–85; to seize goods on ships of king of Vissapore, 94; uncertainty in sailing, 21, 35, 56, 59, 61; under orders of Buckeridge, 91, 94; warned against Persian ships, 95; mentioned, 47, 92
Rebecca, 14
Recovery, 22
Red Sea, 36n, 46, 65, 67, 73
Rice, 7, 23, 30, 31, 35
Roe, Thomas, 9
Roebuck (Utrecht), 50
Rosewater, 24, 27
Rufiji River, 55

St. Christopher le Stocks, 15
St. George Island, 20n
St. Helena, 86
St. James Island, 20
St. Johns. *See* Juan de Nova
St. Lawrence (Madagascar), 10, 19, 59, 84
Saltpeter, 50n
Sandarac (sanderoos), 73
Sanson, Nicholas, 22n
S. Sebastiao fortress, 64n
Save River, 54, 62
Seahorse, 20
Seefa River, 62
Sena, 7, 27, 31, 43, 49, 51, 56, 57, 60, 62, 63, 84
Sena River. *See* Zambezi River
Sheep, 31
Ship tackle: after pump, 77; anchor, 49, 50, 60, 66, 75, 80; best bower, 74; bowsprit, 63; buoy, 74; cable, 49, 50, 76, 78, 80; cable, bass, 66, 74; cable, sheet, 74; capstan, 60, 74; champlats, 78; fish, 63; foresail, 77; grapnel, 66n; gunwale, 77; jury mast, 78; kedge, 74; kellagh, 66, 74, 76; knees, 80; longboat, 60, 77;

mainmast, 77, 78, 80; mainyard, 78; mizzenmast, 77; pintle, 61; rigging, 80; rudder, 56, 61, 78; sails, 80; skiff, 60; spritsail, 77; stanchions, 80; topmast, 80; windlass, 60n; whipstaff, 78
Silver, 7
Siyu, 38n
Slaves: from Assada, 46; from Masseluge, 46; from Quelimane, 43; from Sena, 31, 62; kept by Portuguese at Sena, 31; mentioned, 7, 69
Smirna Merchant, 50
Socotra (Shockatore), 77
Sofala (Cofalla, Soffalla), 32, 43, 44n, 49, 51, 56, 62, 63
Sofala, coast of, 59, 68, 91, 94
Sousa de Távora, Álvaro de, 54
Spanish Armada, 7
Spices, 6, 7
Spirits, 53
Steel, 69
Storms, 11, 56, 57, 60, 61, 63, 68, 76, 77–78, 84
Stringer, Robert, 86
Strong, Peter, 22
Suakin (Swakaine, Swakin), 4, 6
Successe, 36
Sugar, 24, 46
Sumatra, 8
Supply, 52n, 58, 64
Surat (Swally Hole, Swally Marine): Assada refugees at, 10, 58n; blockaded by Dutch, 10; cable and sails from, 80; center of Indian Ocean trade, 4; Dutch and English fighting at, 68; English factory established, 9, 23n; governor of, 29n; president at, 3, 9; trade to Merca, Brava, and Magadoxa, 46; mentioned, 40, 47, 49, 59n, 91, 93, 94, 95

Ta'izz, 4
Tapti River, 23n
Tembe River, 33
Topaz, 86
Tortoise shells, 7, 44, 45, 69, 73
Totty, John, 5
Tourins, 46
Tumbatu Island, 33

United East India Company, 7
United Joint Stock Company, 10
Utrecht (Roebuck), 50n

Verasharoone, 14

Vereenigde Oost-Indische Compagnie, 7
Viages, Don de, 28
Vizapore, king of, 94

Weights and measures, 25, 66
Welcome, 22
Wheat, 30
Wine, 24, 27

Wood, Matthew, 22
Wylde (master of *Lanneret*), 6
Wylde, Charles, 22, 86

Zambezi River (Sena River), 7, 27, 43n, 56, 61n
Zanzibar (Zinzibar, Zanquebar), 33, 44, 71

www.ingramcontent.com/pod-product-compliance
Lightning Source LLC
Chambersburg PA
CBHW061419300426
44114CB00015B/1997